POCKET

BATH, BRISTOL & THE SOUTHWEST

TOP SIGHTS · LOCAL EXPERIENCES

**DAMIAN HARPER, BELINDA DIXON,
OLIVER BERRY**

Contents

Plan Your Trip

Strollers pass Banksy's *Well Hung Lover* (p81)
1000 WORDS/SHUTTERSTOCK ©

Welcome to Bath, Bristol & the Southwest

This is a spectacular region of England, where primordial stone circles hum with energy as ancient Roman baths, serene cathedrals, genteel Georgian cityscapes, colossal bridges and top-drawer museums await exploration. And the great outdoors is never far away, with rugged hikes through sublime moorland or breezy escapades around the Isle of Wight.

Avebury Stone Circle (p113)

Top Sights

Roman Baths

Steaming waters and Roman remains. **p34**

ARIADNA DE RAADT/SHUTTERSTOCK ©

Royal Crescent

Georgian grandeur and everyday life. **p52**

Jane Austen Centre

Austen's regency Bath revealed. **p54**

SS Great Britain

Marvellous, multi-sensory heritage experience. **p70**

TRAVELLIGHT/SHUTTERSTOCK ©

AMY PAY/LONELY PLANET ©

DEATONPHOTOS/SHUTTERSTOCK ©

Bristol Museum & Art Gallery

Ancient artefacts meet street art. **p72**

1000 WORDS/SHUTTERSTOCK ©

NIGEL JARVIS/SHUTTERSTOCK ©

M Shed

Trains, cranes, animation and Banksy. **p74**

Clifton Suspension Bridge

Extraordinary engineering and awesome views. **p92**

Stonehenge

Archaeological mystery, prehistoric monument. **p122**

Glastonbury

Neopagan vibes meet abbey ruins. **p126**

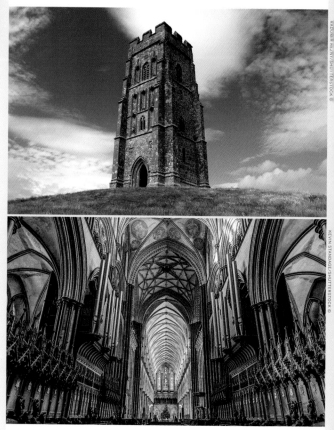

RADUAIR KLZ/KYSHU/ERSTOCK ©

KEVIN STANDAGE/SHUTTERSTOCK ©

Salisbury

Cathedrals, medieval masonry and the Magna Carta. **p106**

Exmoor National Park

Otherworldly landscapes and raw scenery. **p66**

Isle of Wight

Dramatic cliffs and serene sand dunes. **p102**

Eating

The southwest has spearheaded England's culinary renaissance and eateries everywhere fly the flag for local, seasonal, organic produce. The surrounding seas produce just-landed fish, moors and hills provide venison and game, fertile fields add the veg, while harbours and hills add the views.

Gastropubs

While the food in many pubs is good quality and good value, some places raised the bar to such a degree that a whole new genre of eatery – the gastropub – was born. The finest gastropubs are effectively restaurants (with smart decor, neat menus and uniformed table service; a few have won Michelin stars).

Afternoon Tea

An English institution (which locals tend to reserve for special occasions), after-noon tea should be a deeply satisfying affair. A basic minimum should be scones, jam, cream and tea (in a pot, naturally). The best place in Bath to experience it all is the 18th-century setting of the Pump Room Restaurant (p45).

Vegetarians

For vegetarians, many restaurants and pubs have at least one token vegetarian dish, while better places offer much more imaginative choices. Vegans will find the going trickier, except of course at dedicated veggie/vegan restaurants.

By Budget £

Thoughtful Bread Company Quality baking with a slow-food soul. (p42)

Bertinet Bakery French flair and perfect patisserie. (p43)

Fine Cheese Co Deli with a gorgeous selection of cheese and a fine cafe. (p57)

Café Retro A beatnik hangout close to city centre sights. (p44)

Primrose Quality ingredients and old favourites, plus some international surprises; Clifton's favourite cafe. (p98)

Canteen This vibrant community-run cafe-bar is

ANDYPARKER72/SHUTTERSTOCK ©

committed to serving good food at fair prices. (p87)

Small St Espresso The hippest coffeehouse in central Bristol delivers a top-notch caffeine fix. (p77)

St Nicholas Market Only one problem with St Nicks street-food stalls: there's too much choice. (Pictured above; p77)

By Budget ££

Acorn Flavourful, nourishing vegetarian cuisine. (p44)

Pump Room Restaurant The place for an utterly English afternoon tea. (p45)

Scallop Shell Excellent fish dishes and proper chips. (p45)

The Circus Consistently delicious, intensely flavoured food. (p61)

Marlborough Tavern A great bet for gastropub grub. (p63)

Riverstation Almost everything served at this smart eatery, from ice cream to sourdough bread, is homemade. (p86)

Bocabar Stylish Glastonbury restaurant with a winning British menu. (p128)

Fishers Popular with Clifton seafood fans for its impeccably sourced and cooked food. (p99)

Ox A swish restaurant specialising in five choices of steak cut, towering burgers and sticky ribs. (p86)

Thali Café All the flavours and dishes of the Indian subcontinent transplanted to Clifton's hills. (p99)

Shop 3 This epitome of a neighbourhood bistro delights Clifton residents with fine, often-foraged food. (p98)

By Budget £££

Menu Gordon Jones Bath's top table delights diners – one to watch. (p46)

Allium Refined, elaborate dishes – this is stylish cuisine. (p46)

Hudson Steakhouse Perfectly cooked, prime cuts. (p63)

Charter 1227 Classic British cuisine in Salisbury. (p110)

Drinking & Nightlife

Bath boasts some cracking pubs and clubs; the streets to the north and west of the Roman Baths are good places to start explorations. In Bristol, the Floating Harbour and City Dock areas get lively at night, with plenty of bars along Cannon's Rd and the north end of Welsh Back. Clifton also has a good choice of welcoming pubs and bars.

Bars & Pubs

In England, the difference between a bar and a pub is sometimes vague, but generally bars are smarter and louder than pubs, possibly with a younger crowd.

Drinks in English pubs are ordered and paid for at the bar. When it comes to gratuities, it's not usual to tip pub and bar staff.

Beer & Cider

English beer typically ranges from dark brown to bright amber in colour, served at room temperature. Technically it's ale but it's often called 'bitter', to distinguish it from lager, which is generally yellow and served cold.

Beer that's brewed and served traditionally is called 'real ale' to distinguish it from mass-produced brands, and there are many regional varieties. A new breed of microbreweries has sprung up over the last decade, producing their own varieties of traditional and innovative brews, usually referred to as 'craft beers'.

Cider is available sweet or dry and, increasingly, as 'craft cider', often with various fruit or herbal flavours added. Try 'scrumpy', a very strong dry cider traditionally made from local apples.

Tea & Coffee

Although tea is often billed as the national drink, tea consumption fell by around 20% in the five years to 2015, and coffee is becoming ever more popular. The British coffee-shop market is worth almost £8 billion a year, but with the prices some coffee shops charge, maybe that's not surprising.

CHRISTIAN MUELLER/SHUTTERSTOCK ©

Best Pubs

Star A gorgeous old Bath pub positively awash with history, and good beer. (p64)

Salamander The locals head to this cosy nook in Bath for a city-centre pint. (p47)

Bell A proper old pub, beloved by the Bath music crowd. (p64)

Griffin Smart, welcoming and comfortable Bath pub with an excellent choice of beer. (p46)

Haunch of Venison Fourteenth-century Salisbury pub steeped in history, legend and ghosts. (p111)

George & Pilgrim History-infused Glastonbury watering hole. (Pictured above; p129)

Best for Beer

BrewDog Sampler glasses make it tempting to try the offerings at this craft-beer bar. (p77)

Mud Dock Mellow Bristol loft space; local ales and a balcony with water views. (p77)

Star The brewery tap for Bath-based Abbey Ales. (p64)

Amoeba An impossibly large number of spirits and craft beers line this cool Clifton cocktail bar. (p99)

Grain Barge A treat: real ale on a moored-up barge in Bristol with a beer terrace on the roof. (p100)

Best Bars

Amoeba Cool cocktail bar in Clifton for style-conscious drinkers. (p99)

Corkage A wine bar in Bath with a fabulous menu of mini-dishes – come early and stay all night. (p64)

Best Clubs

Thekla Bristol's famous party boat draws the crowds to an eclectic range of club nights. (p88)

Chapel Vibrant and ambitious three-space club in the heart of Salisbury. (p111)

Shopping

Shopping in Bath

Bath's shops are some of the best in the west. The city's main shopping centre is SouthGate (p49), where you'll find all the major chain stores.

High-quality, independent shops line the narrow lanes just north of Bath Abbey and Pulteney Bridge. Milsom St is good for upmarket fashion, while Walcot St has food shops, design stores, vintage-clothing retailers and artisans' workshops.

Shopping in Bristol

High-street chains cluster around **Cabot Circus** (☎0117-952 9361; www.cabotcircus.com; Glass House; ⏱10am-8pm Mon-Sat, 11am-5pm Sun) and Broadmead. The city centre has St Nicholas Market, plus other independent shops dotted around Corn St and Colston St.

Stokes Croft and Gloucester Rd are good for non-chain stores, especially those selling vintage clothing, crafts and second-hand albums.

Clifton is more up-market, with high-end designer, homeware and antiques shops.

Arts & Crafts

Bath Aqua Glass Demonstrations by skilled glassblowers and fiery furnaces make this an atmospheric place to shop. (Pictured above; p57)

Katherine Fraser You're likely to find a weaver at work in this Bath shop that's full of beautiful, bold designs. (p65)

Makers Bristol shop showcasing an excellent range of goods made by local craftspeople. (p88)

Books & Music

Topping & Company
Bookcases so tall that
you need library ladders,
and free coffee – hog
heaven for bibliophiles;
in Bath. (p57)

Stanfords Bristol shop with
a cracking array of travel
books, guides and maps.
(p89)

Resolution Records
Delivers something for both
serious vinyl collectors
and those just wanting to
browse; in Bath. (p49)

Vintage Clothing

Yellow Shop An Aladdin's
cave of all that's vintage and
retro; in Bath. (p65)

Loot It's hipster heaven
in one of Bristol's biggest
vintage stores. (p89)

Dustbowl Clifton shop with
exceptionally good quality
American menswear from
around the 1950s. (p101)

Urban Fox Quality vintage
threads with attitude and
loads of style, located in
Bristol. (p89)

Jemima Rose Top of the
range pre-loved clothes and
designer items; in Clifton.
(p100)

Architecture

Southwest England's architecture spans some five millennia, ranging from Stonehenge to the Clifton Suspension Bridge and beyond. A veritable design timeline can be traced through the architecture of any of England's villages, towns and cities. Prepare for Roman baths, parish churches, magnificent cathedrals, humble cottages and grand, stately homes.

Early Foundations

The oldest surviving structures in England are the grass-covered mounds of earth known as 'tumuli' or 'barrows', used as burial sites by England's prehistoric residents. These mounds are especially common in chalk areas such as Salisbury Plain and the Wiltshire Downs.

The largest and most mysterious chalk mound is Silbury Hill (p113), near Marlborough. Even more impressive than giant tumuli are another legacy of the Neolithic era: menhirs (standing stones), particularly when set out in rings, such as the iconic stone circle of Stonehenge (p122) and the even larger Avebury Stone Circle (p113).

The Roman Era

Roman remains are found in many English towns and cities, but one of the most outstanding pieces of heritage from the era is the lavish Roman spa and bathing complex in Bath (p34). Another fine example from the period is Brading Roman Villa (p103) on the Isle of Wight.

Stately Architecture

A more comfortable and genteel form of their castle forbears, the great stately homes of England display the proportion, symmetry and architectural harmony so in vogue during the 17th and 18th centuries. The styles were later reflected in the fashionable town houses of the Georgian era – most notably in Bath, where the stunning Royal Crescent is the epitome of the genre.

SUE MARTIN/SHUTTERSTOCK ©

Best Historic Architecture

Roman Baths Ancient history; hot, mineral-rich waters; and high-tech displays. (p34)

No 1 Royal Crescent An evocative upstairs-downstairs (gentry and servant) insight into Georgian Bath. (p53)

Royal Crescent One of Britain's most aesthetically pleasing streets. (p52)

The Circus A circle of terraces, where the rich and famous have lived. (p60)

Best Ecclesiastical Architecture

Bath Abbey Soaring architecture, historic tombs and wraparound city views. (p40)

Bristol Cathedral Medieval and Victorian church originally dating to the 12th century. (p80)

Lacock Abbey Intriguing former Augustinian nunnery in the medieval Wiltshire village of Lacock. (Pictured above; p120)

Best Bridges

Clifton Suspension Bridge Brunel's huge and imposing bridge spanning the Avon Gorge. (p92)

Pulteney Bridge This handsome 18th-century bridge across the River Avon is a landmark in Bath. (p40)

Best Parks & Gardens

Ashton Court Estate A massive and good-looking 344-hectare swath of woodland and parkland. (p99)

Prior Park Fabulous grounds to the south of the centre of Bath. (p45)

Museums

DAVE GOODMAN/SHUTTERSTOCK ©

Best Museums for History

Roman Baths Museum Riveting museum displaying a wealth of Roman artefacts. (p35)

Coleridge Cottage House museum and former home of Samuel Taylor Coleridge. (p137)

Magna Carta One of four surviving copies of the epoch-making document. (p107)

M Shed Terrific museum devoted to the history and people of Bristol. (p74)

Jane Austen Centre Explores the wit, sights and smells of the novelist's time in Bath. (p54)

Salisbury Museum Superb collection of Wiltshire archaeological finds. (p108)

Best Science Museums

We the Curious Fun, educational and interactive learning experience. (p80)

Herschel Museum of Astronomy The Bath home of William Herschel, who first discovered Uranus. (p40)

Fox Talbot Museum Celebrating the English pioneer of the photographic negative, William Henry Fox Talbot. (p120)

Best Architecture Museums

Clifton Suspension Bridge Visitor Centre Get the low-down on Brunel's grade-1 listed bridge over the River Avon. (p93)

Museum of Bath Architecture An A–Z of Bath building styles. (p60)

Best Galleries for Art & Fashion

Victoria Art Gallery Ambitious artistic sweep, with works by Thomas Gainsborough, Walter Sickert and John Nash – plus a program of talks. (p40)

Bristol Museum & Art Gallery From John Constable to Banksy and beyond. (p72)

Fashion Museum Corsets, crinolines, velvet and silk – top-notch, annually changing couture displays. (p60)

Best Museums of Local Culture

Willows & Wetlands Visitor Centre Comprehensive look at the historic willow industry. (p137)

Lake Village Museum Fascinating finds from an ancient bog village; in Glastonbury. (p127)

Best Museums for Transport

Haynes Motor Museum Fantastic collection of cars. (Pictured above; p138)

Fleet Air Arm Museum Step on to the flight deck of a Concorde supersonic passenger airliner. (p138)

Festivals & Events

Bath has a busy program of festivals, with all bookings handled by Bath Festivals (www.bathfestivals.org.uk). Literature lovers will want to be in town during September for the Jane Austen Festival. Bristol likewise has a lively schedule of festivals through summer and autumn. The regional highlight of the year is the Glastonbury Festival.

DFP PHOTOGRAPHIC/SHUTTERSTOCK ©

Bath Comedy Festival (www.bathcomedy.com; ⏱early Apr) A fortnight of jokes, sketches and stand-up comedy.

Bath Festival (www.bath festivals.org.uk; 📞01225-614180; ⏱May) Eclectic and diverse appreciation of art, music, literature and more.

Bath Fringe Festival (www. bathfringe.co.uk; ⏱mid-May–early Jun) Theatre, music, dance and performance festival.

Glastonbury Festival of Contemporary Performing Arts (www.glastonbury festivals.co.uk; tickets from £238; ⏱Jun or Jul) Supreme five-day music and performing-arts festival. (Of Monsters and Men pictured above.)

Bristol Harbour Festival (www.bristolharbourfestival. co.uk; ⏱Jul) A weekend devoted to the city's docks.

Bristol Shakespeare Festival (www.bristolshakes peare.org.uk; ⏱Jul) Summer celebration of the Bard of Avon.

Upfest (www.upfest.co.uk; ⏱Jul) Europe's biggest street-art and graffiti festival; in Bristol.

International Balloon Fiesta (www.bristolballoon fiesta.co.uk; ⏱Aug) Europe's largest hot-air balloon takes to the skies from Bristol.

Great Bath Feast (www. greatbathfeast.co.uk; ⏱Sep) A high point of the foodie calendar.

Jane Austen Festival (www. janeaustenfestivalbath. co.uk; ⏱Sep) Ten days of literary celebration and festivities in Bath.

Encounters (www.encoun ters-festival.org.uk; ⏱Sep) Celebrating short films in Bristol.

Activities

Soak in thermal waters in Bath, tag along on guided tours to clamber up to the roof of Bath Abbey or head out on an acclaimed comedy walk-show around town. Operators also offer cruises up and down the River Avon. In Bristol, guided walks lasso in history, engineering and street art, and you can take a boat trip or a guided foodie bike tour.

TRAVELLIGHT/SHUTTERSTOCK ©

Best Tours

Stone Circle Access Visits
Up-close early morning or evening Stonehenge tours. (p123)

Bath Abbey Tower Tours
Climb the abbey tower and gaze over the countryside from the abbey roof. (p42)

Bristol Street Art Tours
From Banksy classics to great graffiti. (p82)

Clifton Suspension Bridge Tours Popular gratis tours of the vast structure. (p93)

Bizarre Bath Comedy Walk
Offbeat tours around the city. (p41)

High Parts Tour Behind-the-scenes tours of Wells Cathedral. (p133)

Best Boat Trips

Bath City Boat Trips
Fifty-minute trips from the Pulteney Bridge area. (p42)

Bristol Packet Sailings and cruises around the harbour and to the Avon Gorge. (p83)

Best Spas

Thermae Bath Spa Relax in warm Bath waters in a rooftop pool. (p41)

Bristol Lido Water from geothermal springs fill this Victorian outdoor pool. (p97)

Best Hikes & Outdoor Activities

Ridgeway National Trail
Starting near Avebury and running for 87 miles through pastoral Wiltshire. (p115)

Adventurous Activity Company Your chance to climb up and abseil down the plunging Avon Gorge. (p85)

Rocksport Caving and rock climbing in Cheddar Gorge. (Pictured above; p136)

Bloc Climbing and bouldering in the Bristol region. (p85)

SUP Bristol Stand Up Paddleboarding (SUP) around Bristol's waterways. (p85)

For Kids

Both Bath and Bristol have really got their act together for kids. Sights make facts fun; a range of activities – from cookery to theatre – cater to youngsters; and heritage attractions always have kids in mind. Somerset and Wiltshire are more spread out and pastoral, but great for children who like hiking.

URBANBUZZ/SHUTTERSTOCK ©

Top Sights for Kids

SS Great Britain Take the helm and climb the rigging. (Pictured above; p70)

Bristol Museum & Art Gallery Dinosaur skin, a giant biplane and mummified cats, plus learning zones. (p72)

Roman Baths Steaming pools, atmospheric chambers and activity trails, plus a free children's audio tour. (p34)

We the Curious Science meets creativity and play. (p80)

Best for Hands-On Fun

Pump Room Water The hotspring water is free and the sulphureous liquid is likely to induce squeals. (p45)

M Shed Ride on the museum's steam tugs, trains or cranes then embark on the ABC of M Shed. (p74)

Bristol Street Art Tours Fancy being a graffiti artist? Hour-long courses see older kids getting their hands on the cans. (p82)

Child-Friendly Sights

Bristol Zoo Gorillas, monkeys, penguins and seals – and a treetop adventure park. (p97)

Bristol Aquarium Daily talks and feeding demos, plus a collection of sharks, seahorses and rays. (p83)

Active & Outdoors

Adventurous Activity Company For everything from rock climbing and abseiling to canoeing. (p85)

Bath City Sightseeing The chance to ride on an open-topped, red, doubledecker bus. (p49)

Bloc One of the region's best bouldering walls runs special sessions for kids. (p85)

Four Perfect Days

Day 1

Drop by **Bath Abbey** (p40) to pre-book an early afternoon **Tower Tour** (p42), then head to the **Roman Baths** (p34) – give yourself the whole morning to take in the sight. Then drop by the **Pump Room Restaurant** (p45; pictured above) for a free (and warm) glass of the city's fabled spring water.

Return to Bath Abbey to join your Tower Tour. Take a few moments to explore some of the streets around the abbey; they're full of interesting shops.

At **Thermae Bath Spa** (p41) enjoy the massage jets, history-themed steam rooms and naturally heated, alfresco pool. Time your visit to be there at dusk; the city lights look magical across the water.

Day 2

Do a circuit of **The Circus** (p60), then walk west to the **Royal Crescent** (p52) to stroll its entire length, admiring the lawn and Palladian designs.

Continue your 18th- and early-19th-century explorations with several hours at the **Jane Austen Centre** (p54), which outlines the writer's life in Bath and displays dashes of her acerbic wit. The centre's period tearoom is a quaint spot to re-fuel, then head to nearby Gay St and Queen Sq to see some of Austen's former homes.

At Bath's historic **Theatre Royal** (p47; pictured above) bigger productions grace the main stage, while the studio space showcases emerging writers' work. Or catch an art-house flick at the **Little Theatre Cinema** (p37).

Day 3

RUSSELL BINNS/SHUTTERSTOCK ©

Day 4

ADRIAN BAKER/SHUTTERSTOCK ©

In Bristol, drop by **M Shed** (p74) to see Banksy's *Grim Reaper*, *Wallace & Gromit* figurines and slavery displays. By 11am trips on the steam tugs and cranes should be running.

Next ride the steam train that chugs beside the water to the **SS Great Britain** (p70). Walk under the glass 'sea', explore the crew's quarters and then climb the rigging! Afterwards, hunt out Banksy's **Girl with the Pierced Eardrum** (p80) nearby. Stroll back along the quay, pausing at **Mud Dock** (p77; pictured above) for a drink on the water-view balcony.

Sink a drink at **Apple** (p87) – a cider bar in a converted barge, then finish with dancing on the **Thekla** (p88) – Bristol's legendary nightclub boat.

The **Clifton Suspension Bridge** (p92) is first on the day's sightseeing list. Head over to the **visitor centre** (p93) on the opposite bank to discover more about the bridge's intriguing past. Outside, the **Chapter & Holmes** (p98) coffee cart is a top spot to refuel. The **Clifton Observatory & Camera Obscura** (p97; pictured above) provides more cracking bridge views.

Walk off the calories with a stroll to the Bristol Lido. A drink before dinner? The convivial **Albion** (p100) pub is popular with the early-evening crowd.

Stop by **Amoeba** (p99) for one, or several, of its 60 cocktails, then it's off to Clifton's **Bristol Fringe** (p100) for a music gig.

Need to Know

For detailed information, see Survival Guide p141

Currency
Pound Sterling (£)

Language
English

Visas
Generally not required for stays of up to six months. Not a member of the Schengen Zone.

Money
ATMs widely available; credit cards widely accepted.

Time
Britain is on GMT/UTC. The clocks go forward one hour for 'summer time' at the end of March, and go back at the end of October.

Phones
The UK uses the GSM 900/1800 network, which covers the rest of Europe, Australia and New Zealand, but isn't compatible with the North American GSM 1900. Most modern mobiles can function on both networks, but check before you leave home.

Daily Budget

Budget: Less than £70
Dorm bed: £15–36

Double room in hostel: £40

Pizza or pasta: £9–14

Tickets to cheaper museums: £12

Midrange: £70–150
Double room in a B&B: £70–130

Main course in a midrange restaurant: £12–18

Tickets for the big sights: £15–22

Top end: More than £150
Double room in an upmarket hotel: from £135

Three-course meal in restaurant: £30–60

Short-hop taxi fares: £6-8

Useful Websites

Lonely Planet (www.lonelyplanet.com/england) Destination information, hotel bookings, traveller forum and more.

Visit Bath (www.visitbath.co.uk) The city's official visitor site.

The Pig Guide (www.thepigguide.com) Restaurant reviews, news and blogs about Bath's foodie scene.

Visit Bristol (www.visitbristol.co.uk) Bristol's official visitor website.

Bristol 24/7 (www.bristol247.com) Excellent updates covering news, features and what's on in the city.

27

Arriving in Bath, Bristol & the Southwest

✈ Bristol Airport

Bristol Airport is located 8 miles from Bristol and 20 miles from Bath. Destinations in Great Britain and Ireland include Aberdeen, Belfast, Edinburgh, Cork, Glasgow and Newcastle. Direct links with cities in mainland Europe include those to Barcelona, Berlin, Milan and Paris.

🚆 Bath Spa Train Station

Direct connections include London Paddington, Cardiff Central and Bristol. Some intercity connections require a change at Bristol.

🚆 Bristol Temple Meads Train Station

Direct connections include those to London Paddington, Birmingham, Edinburgh and Bath.

🚌 Bath Bus Station

Bath's bus and coach station is near the train station. National Express (www.nationalexpress.com) coaches include connections to London, Heathrow, Bristol and beyond.

🚌 Bristol Bus Station

Bristol's bus station is 500m north of the city centre. National Express (www.nationalexpress.com) has services to London, Heathrow, Bath and beyond.

Getting Around

🚌 Bus

Generally good local services, though Wiltshire's service can be patchy, especially in the northwest.

🚗 Car

The main car-hire firms have offices at the region's airports and main-line train stations.

🚆 Train

Bristol is a main train hub.

Bristol Temple Meads Train Station (p144)

Plan Your Trip Need to Know

CLAUDIO DIVIZIA/SHUTTERSTOCK ©

Bath, Bristol & the Southwest Regions

Clifton (p91)
Handsome Clifton is home to its namesake suspension bridge spanning the spectacular Avon Gorge, and a tempting array of pubs and restaurants.

Bristol City Centre (p69)
Buzzing hub of Bristol, crammed with the picks of the city's top heritage sights, thought-provoking street art and standout restaurants and shops.

Exmoor National Park ◉

Glastonbury ◉

Somerset (p125)
A peaceful corner of England, Somerset eases you into low gear to explore ancient sights, picturesque hills, dramatic gorges and inviting, low-lying wetlands.

Royal Crescent & Northwest Bath (p51)
A delightful confluence of elegant Georgian architecture and Jane Austen culture, with an alluring selection of excellent restaurants and hip cafes.

Central Bath (p33)
Steeped in history, central Bath brings together the incomparable Roman Baths and imposing Bath Abbey, plus a fine crop of dining choices.

Avebury

Stonehenge

Salisbury

Wiltshire (p105)
Wiltshire's captivating pastoral hues and comely villages are matched with the exceptional, ancient sights of Stonehenge and Avebury plus some serene architectural gems.

Isle of Wight

Explore
Bath, Bristol & the Southwest

Bath Abbey (p40) CHRISTIAN MUELLER/SHUTTERSTOCK ©

Explore
Central Bath

Visitors are drawn to central Bath like metal to a magnet. This is the location of the city's ancient historic sights – the Roman Baths and Bath Abbey. Independent stores and smart eateries line the streets fanning out all around – many are pedestrianised and make for vibrant and sophisticated places to stroll.

Central Bath is best explored on foot. Make a beeline to the Roman Baths (p34) and Bath Abbey (p40) – a great tactic to give you more chance of securing a slot on the abbey's superb Tower Tours (p42). Two days gives you more time to do both sights, indulge in a cream tea and head out on a walking tour, while three days could see you also relaxing at Thermae Bath Spa (p41) and tying in a museum or two.

Getting There & Around

🏃 Bath's city centre is just 400m from the bus and train stations.

🚌 Buses 6/6A and 7 run between the bus and train stations and Parade Gardens, which is slightly east of Bath Abbey (£2.50, five minutes, every 15 minutes).

Central Bath Map on p38

The Pump Room (p35) 1000 WORDS/SHUTTERSTOCK ©

Top Sights 📷
Roman Baths

Welcome to one of Northern Europe's significant Roman sites. The elaborate spa complex dates from around 70AD and was known then as Aquae Sulis. Today more than a million visitors a year come to see its historic finds, atmospheric pools and imaginative displays. Best of all you can still sample the waters that drew the Romans here almost 2000 years ago.

◎ MAP P38, D3

📞 01225-477785

www.romanbaths.co.uk

Abbey Churchyard

adult/child/family
£17.50/10.25/48

🕐 9.30am-5pm Nov-Feb, 9am-5pm Mar–mid-Jun, Sep & Oct, 9am-9pm mid-Jun–Aug

Great Bath

This is the heart of the spa complex – a massive, lead-lined pool (pictured left) where hot-spring water stretches between Roman columns and steps lead down from all sides. The niches in the walls would once have been where bathers relaxed. The large flat slab set at an angle across the water inflow is today known as the Diving Stone.

Temple Courtyard

Two thousand years ago, visitors made offerings here at the temple altar. Look out for the digital reconstruction of the temple courtyard, the **Haruspex Stone** (which belonged to a priest) and one of the site's best known finds: **Minerva's Head**.

Sacred Spring

Every day, a whopping 1,170,000 litres of mineral-rich water bubble to the surface through the pool in the centre of this compact courtyard. It's still naturally heated to 46°C (115°F) as it has been for at least 2000 years.

The Pump Room

You can sample the spring water at the Spa Water Fountain in the West Baths, but it's much more atmospheric to head outside and into the Pump Room. This grand Georgian building today houses an elegant restaurant and a traditional fountain dispensing free spring-water samples.

People of Aquae Sulis

Here you'll find tomb statuary, mosaics and the **Beau Street Hoard**, a collection of 17,500 Roman coins dating from between 32 BC and AD 274 found in Bath in eight separate money bags in 2007.

★ Top Tips

o Book fast-track tickets online in advance to dodge the queues.

o Saver tickets cover the Roman Baths and Fashion Museum.

o Free guided tours start on the hour at the Great Bath.

o Admission includes an entertaining audio guide.

✕ Take a Break

The restaurant and tearooms of the Pump Room (p45) are the most atmospheric spot to refuel. Also offering traditional cafe treats is Sally Lunn's (p44), a short walk east.

Walking Tour 🥾

Lazy Days & Sundays

Central Bath sometimes seems awash with visitors. But stepping just a few streets away from the blockbuster sights rewards with mellow ways to get beneath the city's skin. So join the culture-conscious locals as they study artworks, sample regional foods, watch the river traffic and soak in the spa. Much as they have done here for thousands of years.

Walk Facts

Start Thoughtful Bread Company
End Little Theatre Cinema
Length 1.6km

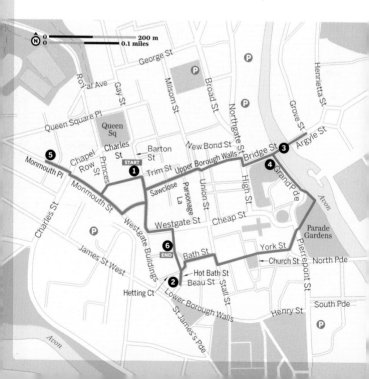

❶ Thoughtful Bread Company

What better place to have a lazy brunch than a slow-food bakery? At Thoughtful Bread (p42) you can sample eggs Benedict or sourdough toast and jam while applauding the firm's eco-credentials. It's strong on foraged ingredients and local sourcing – you might even see some of the regulars bring in their excess fruit and veg and barter it for loaves.

❷ Thermae Bath Spa

A meander through tiny lanes leads to Thermae Bath Spa (p41). Here, 2000 years after the Romans started the trend, soaking in soothing mineral waters is still something the locals love to do. A quick sweat in the sauna and pummel from massage jets, then it's straight to the rooftop pool to see the cityscape through a cloud of steam.

❸ The Avon & Pulteney Bridge

Admiring the views of the River Avon and the thundering weir from Grand Parade is a popular way to pass the time, as is taking a stroll along historic Pulteney Bridge (p40) and browsing its independent shops.

❹ Victoria Art Gallery

The Victoria Art Gallery (p40) isn't on every visitor's itinerary, but it's hugely popular among residents for excellent temporary exhibitions and talks. This could see you learning about anything from the history of entertainment in Bath to the gallery's hidden treasures on an art store tour.

❺ Scallop Shell

As the tour buses depart and the gift shops close, locals head to their favourite eateries. One is the Scallop Shell (p45), which is tucked away from the tourist zone. Here you'll find simple, cheerful decor, supremely fresh fish and shellfish and very happy diners.

❻ Little Theatre Cinema

Bath is a highly cultured place, so no surprise that its inhabitants like to end a lazy day with an art-house film. The **Little Theatre Cinema** (✆ 0871 902 5735; www. picturehouses.com; St Michael's Pl) is hidden away in a lane just off the main tourist drag. This much-loved movie house boasts an art deco interior and plush red seats.

Central Bath

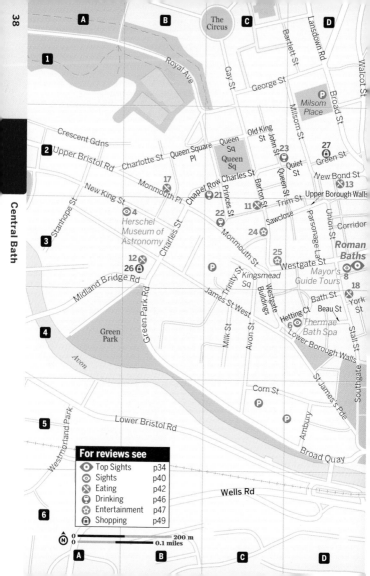

The Circus

Royal Ave

Bartlett St

Lansdown Rd

Walcot St

Gay St

George St

Broad St

Milsom Place

Crescent Gdns

Upper Bristol Rd

Charlotte St

Queen Square Pl

Old King St

John St

Milsom St

27

Green St

23

Queen Sq

Queen Sq

Quiet St

New Bond St

13

New King St

Monmouth Pl

Chapel Row

Charles St

Princes St

Barton St

Queen St

Trim St

Upper Borough Walls

Parsonage Ln

Union St

Corridor

17

21

4

Herschel Museum of Astronomy

22

11

Sawclose

24

Roman Baths

8

12

26

Charles St

Monmouth St

25

Westgate St

Mayor's Guide Tours

18

York St

Midland Bridge Rd

Stanhope St

Green Park Rd

Kingsmead Sq

Trinity St

James St West

Milk St

Avon St

Westgate Buildings

Hetting Ct

Beau St

6

Thermae Bath Spa

Bath St

Stall St

Southgate

Green Park

Avon

Lower Borough Walls

Westmorland Park

Corn St

St James's Pde

Ambury

Lower Bristol Rd

Broad Quay

Wells Rd

For reviews see

N

0 ——— 200 m
0 ——— 0.1 miles

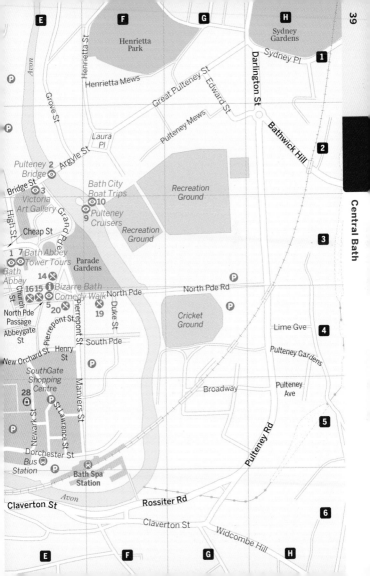

E
F
G
H

Sydney Gardens

Henrietta Park

Sydney Pl **1**

Avon

Henrietta St

Henrietta Mews

Great Pulteney St

Edward St

Darlington St

Bathwick Hill **2**

Grove St

Laura Pl

Pulteney Mews

Pulteney **2** Bridge

Argyle St

Bridge St

Bridge St **3**

Victoria Art Gallery

Grand Pde

Bath City Boat Trips **10**

Recreation Ground

3

High St

9 Pulteney Cruisers

Recreation Ground

Cheap St

1 7 Bath Abbey Tower Tours

Bath Abbey

Parade Gardens

North Pde Rd **P**

14

16 15 Bizarre Bath
Comedy Walk

North Pde

North Pde Road

Cricket Ground **P**

Church St

5

20

19

Duke St

Lime Gve **4**

North Pde Passage

Pierrepont St

South Pde

Pulteney Gardens

Abbeygate St

New Orchard St

Henry St

P

Manvers St

Broadway

Pulteney Ave

Pulteney Rd **5**

SouthGate Shopping Centre

28

P

St Lawrence St

Newark St

P

Dorchester St

Bus Station **P**

Bath Spa Station

Avon

Rossiter Rd

Claverton St

Claverton St

Widcombe Hill **6**

H

E
F
G

P **P**

Sights

Bath Abbey   CHURCH

1 MAP P38, E3

Looming above the city centre, Bath's huge abbey church was built between 1499 and 1616, making it the last great medieval church raised in England. Its most striking feature is the west facade, where angels climb up and down stone ladders, commemorating a dream of the founder, Bishop Oliver King. Tower tours (p42) leave on the hour from Monday to Friday, and every half-hour on Saturdays. Tours can only be booked at the Abbey shop, on the day. (01225-422462; www.bathabbey.org; Abbey Churchyard; suggested donation adult/child £4/2; 9.30am-5.30pm Mon, 9am-5.30pm Tue-Fri, to 6pm Sat, 1-2.30pm & 4.30-6pm Sun)

Pulteney Bridge   BRIDGE

2 MAP P38, E2

Elegant Pulteney Bridge has spanned the River Avon since the late 18th century and continues to be a much-loved and much-photographed Bath landmark (the view from Grand Parade, southwest of the bridge, is the best). Browse the shops that line both sides of the bridge or have a rest and a Bath bun in the Bridge Coffee Shop.

Victoria Art Gallery   MUSEUM

3 MAP P38, E2

Bath's second-most-visited museum has collections that include everything from Turner and Gainsborough to contemporary art. The programme of temporary exhibitions (adult/child £4.50/free) and talks is particularly strong. (01225-477233; www.victoriagal.org.uk; Bridge St; admission free; 10.30am-5.30pm)

Herschel Museum of Astronomy   MUSEUM

4 MAP P38, B3

In 1781 astronomer William Herschel discovered Uranus from the garden of his home, now converted into a museum. Herschel shared

---

Bath's Hot Springs

The hot springs that bubble up in Bath at 46°C (115°F) fell as rain some 10,000 years ago. It drained down more than a mile to be heated by the earth's forces and pushed back up, including sulphate, calcium, chloride and iron.

The best places to get to grips with this heritage are to tour the Roman Baths (p34) complex and head for its modern-day incarnation – the steam rooms and pool of Thermae Bath Spa. You can also ask for a free drink of spa water at the Pump Room Restaurant (p45).

the house with his wife, Caroline, also an important astronomer. Their home is little changed since the 18th century; an astrolabe in the garden marks the position of the couple's telescope. (☏01225-446865; www.herschelmuseum.org.uk; 19 New King St; adult/child £6.50/3.20; ⏰11am-5pm Jul & Aug, 1-5pm Mon-Fri, 10am-5pm Sat & Sun Mar-Jun & Sep)

Bizarre Bath Comedy Walk

WALKING

5 ⊙ MAP P38, E4

A fabulously daft city tour mixing street theatre and live performance that bills itself as 'hysterical rather than historical'. Leaves nightly from outside the tourist office on North Pde Passage.

There's no need to book. (www.bizarrebath.co.uk; adult/student £10/7; ⏰8pm Apr-Oct)

Thermae Bath Spa

SPA

6 ⊙ MAP P38, D4

Taking a dip in the Roman Baths might be off limits, but you can still sample the city's curative waters at this fantastic modern spa complex, housed in a shell of local stone and plate glass. The showpiece is the open-air rooftop pool, where you can bathe in naturally heated, mineral-rich waters with a backdrop of Bath's cityscape – a don't-miss experience, best enjoyed at dusk. (☏01225-331234; www.thermaebathspa.com; Hot Bath St; spa £36-40, treatments from £65; ⏰9am-9.30pm, last entry 7pm)

West facade, Bath Abbey

American Museum in Britain

Britain's largest collection of American folk art, including First Nations textiles, patchwork quilts and historic maps, is housed in a fine **mansion** (📞01225-460503; www. americanmuseum.org; Claverton Manor; adult/child £12.50/7; ⏰10am-5pm Tue-Sun late Mar–Oct) a couple of miles from the city centre. Several rooms have been decorated to resemble a 17th-century Puritan house, an 18th-century tavern and a New Orleans bedroom c 1860. A free shuttle bus (11.40am to 5pm) leaves from Terrace Walk, beside Parade Gardens.

Bath Abbey Tower Tours

TOURS

7 ◉ MAP P38, E3

The 50-minute tours of Bath Abbey's tower (p40) see you standing above the abbey's fan-vaulted ceiling, sitting behind the clock face and visiting the ringing and bell chamber. The views from the roof of the city and surrounding countryside are superb. Tours can only be booked at the Abbey shop, on the day only. (📞01225-422462; www.bathabbey.org; adult/child £8/4; ⏰10am-5pm Apr-Aug, 10am-4pm Sep & Oct, 11am-4pm Nov-Mar, closed Sun)

Mayor's Guide Tours

WALKING

8 ◉ MAP P38, D3

Excellent historical tours provided free by the Mayor's Corp of Honorary Guides; tours cover about 2 miles and are wheelchair accessible. They leave from within the Abbey Churchyard, outside the Pump Room. There are extra tours at 7pm on Tuesdays and Thursdays May to August. (www.bathguides.org. uk; admission free; ⏰10.30am & 2pm Sun-Fri, 10.30am Sat)

Pulteney Cruisers

BOATING

9 ◉ MAP P38, F3

Runs between five and 11 hour-long boat trips on the River Avon each day. (📞01225-863600; www. bathboating.com; Pulteney Bridge; adult/child £9/4; ⏰mid-Mar–Oct)

Bath City Boat Trips

BOATING

10 ◉ MAP P38, F3

Various boat operators cruise the River Avon. This company runs 50-minute trips from the Pulteney Bridge area. (📞07980 335185; www. bathcityboattrips.com; Pulteney Sluice Gate; adult/child £11/9)

Eating

Thoughtful Bread Company

BAKERY £

11 ✗ MAP P38, C3

Come lunchtime, people could well be queuing out the door of this snug artisan bakery, where chunky loaves sit alongside delicate macaroons and salted-caramel bombs. It also has a stall at Bath's Saturday farmers market – come early as it sells out fast. (☎01225-471747; www.thethought fulbreadcompany.com; 19 Barton St; ⏱8am-5pm Tue-Fri, 8am-4pm Sat & Sun)

Farmers Market
MARKET £

12 MAP P38, B3

Excellent farmers market held on Saturday mornings inside Green Park Station – a disused railway hall. (www.greenparkstation.co.uk; Green Park; ⏱9am-1.30pm Sat)

Bertinet Bakery
BAKERY £

13 MAP P38, D2

The flavourful fillings and light pastry of the pasties at baker

Museum Discounts

Saver tickets covering the Roman Baths and the Fashion Museum cost adult/child/family £22.50/12.25/58.

There is also a joint ticket (adult/child/family £17/8/40) covering Beckford's Tower, No 1 Royal Crescent, the Museum of Bath Architecture and the Herschel Museum of Astronomy.

Richard Bertinet's take-out shop could change your view of that foodstuff for good. You also might find yourself tempted by rich quiches, cheese-studded croissants, French-inspired cakes and irresistible pistachio swirls.

Pulteney Bridge (p40) on the River Avon

(www.bertinet.com/bertinetbakery;
1 New Bond St Pl; baked goods £2.50-
5; ⊙8am-5pm Mon-Fri, 8.30am-
5.30pm Sat)

Café Retro

CAFE £

14 🍴 MAP P38, E3

A poke in the eye for the corporate coffee chains. The paint job's scruffy, the crockery's ancient and none of the furniture matches, but that's all part of the charm. This is a cafe from the old school, and there are few places better for burgers, croques or cake. Takeaways (in biodegradable containers) are available from Retro-to-Go next door. (📞01225-339347; www.caferetro.co.uk; 18 York St; mains £5-10; ⊙9am-5pm; 🛜)

Sally Lunn's

CAFE £

15 🍴 MAP P38, E4

Eating a bun at Sally Lunn's is a Bath tradition. It's all about proper English tea here, brewed in bone-china teapots, with finger sandwiches and dainty cakes served by waitresses in frilly aprons. (📞01225-461634; www.sallylunns.co.uk; 4 North Pde Passage; mains £6-17, afternoon tea £8-40; ⊙10am-9pm)

Acorn

VEGETARIAN ££

16 🍴 MAP P38, E4

Proudly proclaiming 'plants taste better', Bath's premier vegetarian restaurant tempts you inside with aromas reflecting its imaginative, global-themed cuisine. The wine flights (two/three courses

Prior Park

SCION CREATIVE/SHUTTERSTOCK ©

Prior Park

Partly designed by the landscape architect Lancelot 'Capability' Brown, the grounds of this 18th-century **estate** (NT; ☎01225-833977; www.nationaltrust.org.uk; Ralph Allen Dr; adult/child £7.40/3.70; ⊙10am-5.30pm daily Feb-Oct, 10am-4pm Sat & Sun Nov-Jan) on Bath's southern fringe feature cascading lakes and a graceful Palladian bridge, one of only four such structures in the world (look out for the period graffiti, some of which dates back to the 1800s).

The estate was established by the entrepreneur Ralph Allen, who made his fortune founding Britain's first postal service, and who owned many of the local quarries from which the city's amber-coloured Bath stone was mined. The house itself is now occupied by a private school, but there are several lovely pathways around the estate, including the Bath Skyline, a 6-mile circular trail offering truly inspirational views.

The park is located a mile south of Bath's centre. Bus 2 (every 30 minutes) stops nearby, as does Bath City Sightseeing's 'City Skyline' tour.

£15/22) matched to the set dinner menus are good value; or opt for a pear Bellini (£7) to get the liquid refreshments under way. (☎01225-446059; www.acornvegetariankitchen.co.uk; 2 North Pde Passage; lunch 2/3 courses £18/23, dinner 2/3 courses £28/37; ⊙noon-3pm & 5.30-9.30pm, to 3.30pm & 10pm Sat; 🖋)

Scallop Shell   FISH & CHIPS ££

17 ❌ MAP P38, B2

One of Bath's best fish eateries is also one of its simplest – bags of potatoes piled up beside the door and plain wooden tables. The theme continues with the food – unfussy and unafraid to let the freshness of the ingredients and the quality of the cooking speak for themselves. (☎01225-420928; www.thescallopshell.co.uk; 22 Monmouth Pl; mains £10-15; ⊙noon-9.30pm Mon-Sat)

Pump Room Restaurant   CAFE ££

18 ❌ MAP P38, D4

Elegance is everywhere in this tall, Georgian room, from the string trio and Corinthian columns to the oil paintings and glinting chandeliers. It sets the scene perfectly for morning coffee, classic lunches and the dainty sandwiches and cakes of its famous afternoon tea (£26 to £35 per

Menu Gordon Jones

If you enjoy dining with an element of surprise, then **Menu Gordon Jones** (☎01225-480871; www.menugordonjones.co.uk; 2 Wellsway; 5-course lunch £50, 6-course dinner £55; ⏰12.30-2pm & 7-9pm Tue-Sat) will be right up your culinary boulevard. Menus are dreamt up daily and showcase the chef's taste for experimental ingredients (expect mushroom mousse and Weetabix ice cream) and eye-catching presentation (test tubes and paper bags). It's superb value given the skill on show. Reservations essential. The wines are all organic and biodynamic.

person). (☎01225-444477; www.romanbaths.co.uk; Stall St; snacks £7-9, mains £13-17; ⏰9.30am-5pm)

Sotto Sotto   ITALIAN ££

19 🍴 MAP P38, F4

The setting – an artfully lit vaulted brick chamber – is superb, and the food matches it for style. Authentic Italian dishes include choices such as herb-crusted lamb in a rich red wine sauce, and sweet potato gnocchi with fresh sea bass. Top tip: don't forgo the garlicky, sautéed-spinach side. (☎01225-330236; www.sottosotto.co.uk; 10 North Pde; mains £11-25; ⏰noon-2pm & 5-10pm)

Allium   MODERN BRITISH £££

20 🍴 MAP P38, E4

At the Abbey Hotel you'll find fine dining inside a Best Western Hotel. Head chef Rupert Taylor's work at an array of multi-Michelin-starred restaurants influences his cuisine here – it's awash with emulsions and purées and foams, and showcases seasonal ingredients. The signature dish of venison rolled in hay ash lives up to the hype. (☎01225-461603; www.abbeyhotelbath.co.uk/allium; North Pde; lunch & early-evening 2/3 courses £20/25, dinner mains £20-26; ⏰7-10am, noon-3pm & 5.30-9pm)

Drinking

Colonna & Smalls   CAFE

21 ☕ MAP P38, C2

If you're keen on caffeinated beans, this is a cafe not to miss. A mission to explore coffee means there are three guest espresso varieties and smiley staff happy to share their expertise. They'll even tell you that black filter coffee – yes, filter coffee – is actually the best way to judge high-grade beans. (☎07766 808067; www.colonnaandsmalls.co.uk; 6 Chapel Row; ⏰8am-5.30pm Mon-Fri, from 8.30am Sat, 10am-4pm Sun; 📶)

Griffin   PUB

22 ☕ MAP P38, C3

Duck into this smart, friendly pub to find a wealth of beers and ciders, polished floors and the kind of leather armchairs you don't want to leave. Ideal for staying for food (noon to 2pm and 6pm to 9pm Wednesday to Saturday, mains £7 to £16), including smoked eel and homemade Scotch eggs. (☏01225-420919; www.thegriffinbath.co.uk; Monmouth St; ⏰noon-11pm Mon-Sat, to 10.30pm Sun; 📶)

Salamander   PUB

23 🍺 MAP P38, C2

Owned by Bath Ales, locals' fa-vourite 'the Sally' quenches many a thirst with house beers such as amber Gem and the stronger Wild Hare Pale Ale. Food is served upstairs in the dining room. (☏01225-428889; www.bathales.com; 3 John St; ⏰11am-11pm Sun-Thu, to 1am Fri & Sat; 📶)

Entertainment

Theatre Royal   THEATRE

24 ⭐ MAP P38, C3

Bath's historic theatre dates back 200 years. Major touring productions appear in the main auditorium and smaller shows take place in the Ustinov Studio. (☏01225-448844; www.theatreroyal. org.uk; Sawclose)

Komedia   COMEDY

25 ⭐ MAP P38, C3

Renowned comedy venue featur-ing touring shows and the sell-out Krater Saturday Comedy Club. Also live music, bingo and discos. (☏01225-489070; www.komedia. co.uk; 22-23 Westgate St)

History of Bath

Legend has it that King Bladud, a Trojan refugee and father of King Lear, founded Bath some 2800 years ago when his pigs were cured of leprosy by a dip in the muddy swamps. The Romans established the town of Aquae Sulis in AD 44 and built the extensive baths com-plex and a temple to the goddess Sulis-Minerva.

In 944 a monastery was founded on the site of the present abbey, helping Bath's development as an ecclesiastical centre and wool-trading town. But it wasn't until the early 18th century that Ralph Allen and the celebrated dandy Richard 'Beau' Nash made Bath the centre of fashionable society. Allen developed the quarries at Coombe Down, constructed Prior Park and employed the two John Woods (father and son) to create Bath's signature buildings.

During WWII, Bath was hit by the Luftwaffe during the so-called Baedeker raids, which targeted historic cities in an effort to sap British morale. In 1987, Bath became the only city in Britain to be declared a Unesco World Heritage Site in its entirety.

Ceiling of Bath Abbey (p40)

Bath Guided Tours

Ranks of providers are lining up to help you discover Bath, on foot, by boat and by bus. They offer an excellent way to get extra insights into the city before embarking on your own explorations.

The pick of the tours sees you scaling hundreds of steps up the staircases of Bath Abbey (p42) via the top of the fan-vaulted ceiling and bell chamber to the roof.

The best heritage-themed walking tours are the superb – and free – strolls of the Mayor's Guide Tours (p42), which cover 2 miles and take in all the main sights. The award-winning Bizarre Bath Comedy Walk (p41) is a hilarious city highlight, but don't expect much history. The boats that set off from the weir near Pulteney Bridge for hour-long cruises offer a different perspective of the city – the main operators are Bath City Boat Trips (p42) and Pulteney Cruisers (p42).

Or you can see the city by open-topped bus. The **Bath City Sightseeing** (Bath Bus Company; ☏ 01225-444102; www.bathbuscompany.com; adult/child/family £15/9.50/43; ☺ 10am-5pm, reduced services Jan-Mar) hop-on/hop-off service has two routes: the City Tour, which takes in the centre and the Royal Crescent, and the Skyline Tour, which goes as far as Prior Park.

Shopping

Resolution Records MUSIC

26 🔒 MAP P38, B3

Among the ranks of vinyl LPs and 45s here you'll find everything from hip hop and funk to '60s beat, Joni Mitchell and The Who. Prices range from £1 a disc to pristine collectors' items fetching up to £60. (www.resolutionrecords.co.uk; Green Park Market; ☺ 10am-5pm Mon-Sat, to 4pm Sun)

Tasting Room WINE

27 🔒 MAP P38, D2

There's a cosy, neighbourhood feel in this bijou wine shop, which also offers wine tasting by the glass. There may only be two or three vintages available for sampling at any one time, but they'll be top class. (☏ 01225-483070; www.tastingroom.co.uk; 6 Green St; ☺ 9.30am-5.30pm Mon-Thu, to 6pm Fri & Sat)

SouthGate SHOPPING CENTRE

28 🔒 MAP P38, E5

Bath's smart, modern, open-plan shopping centre has all of the major chain stores. (www.southgatebath.com; ☺ 9am-6pm Mon-Wed, Fri & Sat, 9am-7pm Thu, 11am-5pm Sun)

Explore

Royal Crescent & Northwest Bath

Two things draw most visitors to northwest Bath: exquisite architecture and literary links – this is the home of the grand sweep of the Royal Crescent, the circular Circus and the Jane Austen Centre. Walcot St offers artisan workshops and retro stores, while a scattering of on-trend cafes, live-music venues and bars see Bath's hipsters heading here for a night out.

A well-trodden trail leads from the Roman Baths and Bath Abbey up streets lined with chichi shops to the Circus (p60) and then to the start of the Royal Crescent (p52). Heading straight into No 1 Royal Crescent ensures you get plenty of background about the curving terrace before you stroll along its length. From there, heading back via the Georgian Garden (p61) and the Jane Austen Centre (p54) is a popular approach. You can manage to see all of these sights in a day, before heading to the neighbourhood's restaurants, clubs and bars.

Getting There & Around

🚶 The Royal Crescent is around 1 mile from Bath's bus and train stations. The Circus is some 600m from the Roman Baths and Bath Abbey.

🚌 Take bus 6 or 7 from the train station to the Alfred St stop on Lansdown Rd; the Circus is a 200m walk west from there. Bath City Sightseeing buses run here.

Royal Crescent & Northwest Bath Map on p58

Georgian Garden (p61) HILDAWEGES PHOTOGRAPHY/GETTY IMAGES ©

Top Sights
Royal Crescent

Even without Bath's famous Roman Baths, the Royal Crescent would put the city high on any must-visit British locations list. The construction in the 1700s of this spectacular architectural set piece both signalled Bath's status as an ultra-fashionable destination and ensured it continued. Today No 1 Royal Crescent also sees you exploring the interior of an authentically restored Georgian home.

◎ MAP P58, B3

The Architecture

The vast sweep of the Royal Crescent is an imposing, curving terrace of 30, four-story mansions that overlook a private park. They were designed by John Wood the Younger, with construction beginning in 1767. From the front the houses are identical – features to look out for include the two-story Ionic columns, with a strip of Palladian moldings above, and the ha-ha (hidden ditch) that separates the public park from the gardens used by the Crescent's residents.

No 11 Royal Crescent

Track down the plaque at No 11 Royal Crescent. It outlines events worthy of a Jane Austen plot – the elopement of 18-year-old Elizabeth Linley with the playwright Richard Sheridan. He became famous. She died, disappointed and consumptive, aged 38.

No 1 Royal Crescent: Upstairs

At the eastern edge of the Crescent sits a superb, and rare, insight into life inside a Georgian mansion. **No 1 Royal Crescent** (www.no1royal crescent.org.uk; ☎ 01225-428126; adult/child/family £10.30/5.10/25.40; ◷ 10am-5pm) was the first of the houses to be built in the terrace, and was the home of Henry Sandford and his servants. The fabrics, paintings and furniture are all authentic. You'll tour around 20 rooms, including the parlour, complete with newspapers; gentleman's retreat, featuring a desk globe; dining room, set for an elaborate dinner; and lady's bedchamber – here spot the wig scratcher that provided relief from headlice.

No 1 Royal Crescent: Downstairs

Life below stairs at No 1 is well represented: the servants' hall, with plain pewter plates; the housekeeper's room, complete with ledger and bills; and the kitchen with wooden racks to hang hams.

★ Top Tips

○ Saver tickets cover No 1 Royal Crescent and the Museum of Bath Architecture.

○ Last entry to No 1 Royal Crescent is an hour before closing.

○ To get a real feel for the sheer scale of the Royal Crescent, stroll to the grass beneath the private lawns.

✖ Take a Break

The chic Circus bistro (p61) is on the road leading onto the Royal Crescent.

The Adventure Cafe Bar (p57) is an excellent, laid-back eating option some 10 minutes' walk east of the Royal Crescent.

Top Sights 📷
Jane Austen Centre

Jane Austen is arguably Bath's best-known former resident. She set two of her novels here, lived in the city from 1801 to 1806 and visited regularly. The exhibits in the Jane Austen Centre chart the course of her stays in the city, revealing how the observations she made then about Regency society were key themes in her work. Costumed characters help keep things fun.

◎ MAP P58, E5

📞 01225-443000

www.janeausten.co.uk

40 Gay St

adult/child £12/6.20

🕐 9.45am-5.30pm Apr-Oct, 10am-4pm Sun-Fri, 9.45am-5.30pm Sat Nov-Mar

The Bath Novels

Bath is the main setting of *Northanger Abbey* and *Persuasion*. Panels explore the plot lines of both with well-chosen snippets of text detailing how different characters felt about the city. A sense of the writer's feelings about the spa town she sometimes found stultifying also emerges, thanks to juxtapositions of sections from Austen's letters and the depictions of her characters' activities, such as taking long walks in the surrounding countryside, dancing, flirting and visiting the Pump Room, which all help bring the period city to life.

Austen's Bath

Maps detail the houses that Austen lived in in Bath. One is just a few doors away from the centre, which is itself set in a Georgian town-house. Witty excerpts from the writer's letters reveal her views of the properties she stayed at and the people she stayed with. A theme that's also strong in her writing emerges: social status determines and is revealed by where you can afford to live – that famous Austen preoccupation with 'incomes per year'.

Hands-On Exhibits

The tastes, smells and conventions of Regency Bath are conveyed thanks to the Bath Oliver biscuits you can taste (think plain, dry crackers); 'Scents & Sensibility', in which rose water, orange blossom and lavender conjure up how her female characters would have smelled; mystery objects, including a herb cutter, candle snuffer and glove stretcher; and Language of the Fan, where you can practise sending amorous, coded messages through accessory positioning. You can even write with quill and ink – scratchy and surprisingly difficult.

★ Top Tips

o The attraction tends to be less crowded in the morning.

o An Early Bird online ticket saves £1 per adult on visits before noon.

o The costumed guides, all characters from Austen's novels, are happy to share more background information.

o Show your admission ticket to get 10% off in the gift shop and tearoom.

✖ Take a Break

The centre's Regency Tea Room serves up traditional snacks in period style.

Feel like something more modern? Try the soups and sarnies at the Thoughtful Bread Company (p42).

Royal Crescent & Northwest Bath   Jane Austen Centre

Walking Tour 🥾

Hip Hang-Outs & Cool Shops

From the Romans to Jane Austen via the Georgians, Bath is (rightly) famous for its rich past. But hidden in among all that heritage is a cool, contemporary city of trendy cafes and hip bars. That's especially true in northern Bath, where snappy dressers sip espressos and craft cocktails after scouring vintage shops for those one-off items that'll keep them firmly on-trend.

Walk Facts

Start Fine Cheese Co
End Circo
Length 1km

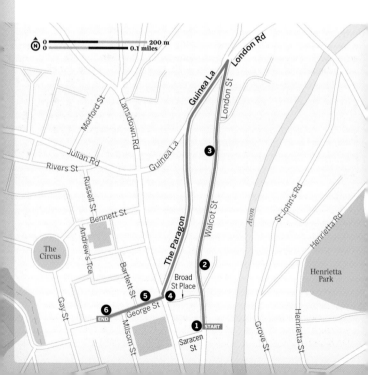

❶ Fine Cheese Co

You don't have to like cheese to love the **Fine Cheese Co** (📞01225-448748; www.finecheese.co.uk; 31 Walcot St; snacks from £4; 🕑9am-5pm Mon-Sat), the exquisite pastries, punchy coffee and creative lunchtime specials ensure this cafe-deli has a passionate local following. And because it's set at the foot of Walcot St, it's the perfect launch-pad for counterculture explorations.

❷ Walcot St

Walcot St is Bath's self-styled Artisan Quarter and while you won't be knee deep in crafts, there are enough workshops, eateries and independent retailers to beckon you this way. The Yellow Shop (p65) is a treasure trove for all that's vintage, retro and new, while at Katherine Fraser (p65) you get to see an artisan weaver at work and browse the beautiful, bold designs.

❸ Bath Aqua Glass

The fierce heat from the furnaces means the street door is normally open at the Bath Aqua Glass **workshop** (Theatre of Glass; 📞01225-428146; www.bathaquaglass.com; 105 Walcot St; 🕑10am-5pm Mon-Sat), providing views of skilled craftspeople rolling, dipping and blowing molten materials into aquamarine designs. It's well worth heading into the shop or watching a demonstration (adult/child £2.50/1.50, at 11.15am and 2.15pm Monday to Saturday) for a close-up insight into the glass-blowers' skills.

❹ Topping & Company

A firm favourite with Bath's bibliophiles, **Topping & Company** (📞01225-428111; www.toppingbooks.co.uk; The Paragon; 🕑8.30am-7.30pm) has an impressive 50,000 titles on display, accessed by rolling library ladders. It's the kind of place you can happily linger in for hours – a feeling that's helped by the free tea and proper coffee on offer.

❺ Adventure Cafe Bar

Whatever time of day you hit the **Adventure Cafe Bar** (📞01225-462038; www.adventurecafebar.co.uk; 5 Princes Bldgs, George St; mains £5-10; 🕑8am-3am Mon-Fri, from 9am Sat & Sun; 🛜🍴), you'll probably find something to suit – brunch is served till noon, from there it's a seamless culinary saunter to lunch and dinner, beer and cocktails, making it a hip hangout with substance as well as style.

❻ Circo

When a place is hidden away it tends to attract locals who are in the know. That's true of **Circo** (📞01225-585100; www.circobar.co.uk; 15 George St; 🕑5-11.45pm Tue-Thu, to 3am Fri & Sat), an upscale bar that stages regular live music, boutique cinema screenings, gin tastings and cocktail masterclasses. You'll find it down some stairs at the end of a passageway. It's worth the steps.

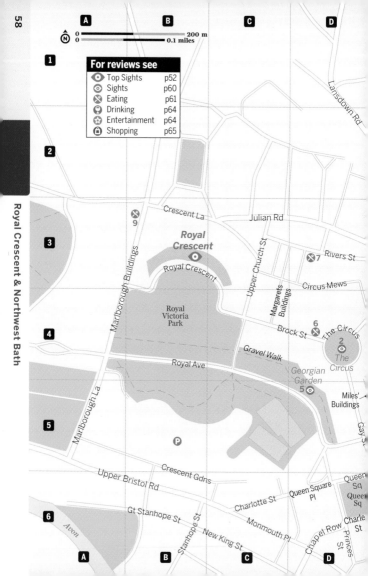

N

0   200 m
0   0.1 miles

For reviews see

- Top Sights   p52
- Sights   p60
- Eating   p61
- Drinking   p64
- Entertainment   p64
- Shopping   p65

Lansdown Rd

Crescent La

Julian Rd

Royal Crescent

9

Royal Crescent

Marlborough Buildings

Upper Church St

Rivers St
7

Margarets Buildings

Circus Mews

Royal Victoria Park

Brock St

6

The Circus

2
The Circus

Gravel Walk

Royal Ave

Georgian Garden
5

Miles' Buildings

Marlborough La

Gay St

P

Crescent Gdns

Upper Bristol Rd

Charlotte St

Queen Square Pl

Queen Sq

Queen Sq

Avon

Gt Stanhope St

Stanhope St

New King St

Monmouth Pl

Chapel Row

Charle St

Princes St

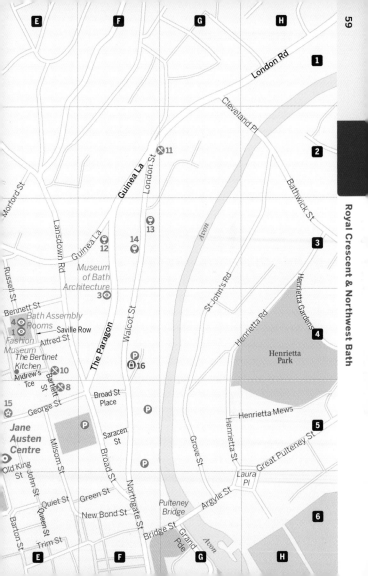

E **F** **G** **H**

London Rd

1

Cleveland Pl

2

Bathwick St

Guinea La

London St

🍴 11

Morford St

Lansdown Rd

Guinea La

Avon

3

🍷 13

Henrietta Gardens

🏪 12

14 🛏

St John's Rd

Museum
of Bath
Architecture

Walcot St

Henrietta Rd

3 ◉

Russell St

Bennett St

4

Bath Assembly
Rooms

4 ◉
1 ◉

Fashion
Museum

Saville Row

Alfred St

The Paragon

P
🔒 16

Henrietta Park

The Bertinet
Kitchen

Henrietta Mews

Andrew's
Tce

🏪 10

Bartlett St

🏪 8

5

15 ✪

George St

Broad St
Place

P

Henrietta St

Great Pulteney St

Milsom St

Jane
Austen
Centre

P

Saracen
St

Grove St

Broad St

P

Laura
Pl

Old King
St

John St

Quiet St

Green St

Northgate St

Pulteney
Bridge

Argyle St

6

Queen St

New Bond St

Barton St

Trim St

Bridge St

Grand
Pde

Avon

E **F** **G** **H**

Sights

Fashion Museum
MUSEUM

1 ◉ MAP P58, E4

The world-class collections on display in this museum, within the basement of the city's Georgian Assembly Rooms, include costumes from the 17th to late-20th centuries. Some exhibits change annually; check the website for the latest. (☏01225-477789; www.fashionmuseum. co.uk; Assembly Rooms, 19 Bennett St; adult/child £9/7; ⏱10.30am-5pm Mar-Oct, to 4pm Nov-Feb)

The Circus
ARCHITECTURE

2 ◉ MAP P58, D4

The Circus is a Georgian masterpiece. Built to John Wood the Elder's design and completed in 1768, it's said to have been inspired by the Colosseum in Rome. Arranged over three equal terraces, the 33 mansions form a circle and overlook a grassy disc populated by plane trees. Famous residents have included Thomas Gainsborough, Clive of India, David Livingstone and the actor Nicholas Cage.

Museum of Bath Architecture
MUSEUM

3 ◉ MAP P58, F4

The stories behind the building of Bath's most striking structures are explored here, using antique tools, displays on Georgian construction methods and a 1:500 scale model of the city. (☏01225-333895; www. museumofbatharchitecture.org.uk;

The Circus

Jane Austen in Bath

Bath seizes every opportunity to celebrate its links with Jane Austen. The author of *Pride and Prejudice* and *Sense and Sensibility* is famous for her wry sideswipes at Georgian and Regency society.

Having stayed at No 13 Queen Square in 1799, the family moved to No 4 Sydney Pl at the end of Great Pulteney St in 1801 when her father retired. After Mr Austen died in 1805 the family moved to a succession of rented homes, each of lower status than the last – around Green Park, at 25 Gay St and in Trim St.

Austen set *Northanger Abbey* and *Persuasion* in Bath. Fans will enjoy scouring those novels for references to recognisable buildings, streets and hills, and for her caustic references to spa-town sensibilities. Her Bath letters reveal a woman who was also touchingly wearied by damp basements and high rents.

The Jane Austen Centre (p54) provides a good introduction to the writer's life in the city; it and the tourist office sell an informative *Map of Bath in the Time of Jane Austen* (£4).

The Vineyards, off the Paragon; adult/child £5.50/2.50; ⏰2-5pm Tue-Fri, 10.30am-5pm Sat & Sun mid-Feb–Nov)

Bath Assembly Rooms
HISTORIC BUILDING

4 ◉ MAP P58, E4

When they opened in 1771, the city's stately Assembly Rooms were where fashionable Bath socialites gathered to waltz, play cards and listen to the latest chamber music. Today they're unfurnished; rooms that are open to the public include the Great Octagon, tearoom and ballroom – all lit by their original 18th-century chandeliers. (NT; ☎01225-477786; www.nationaltrust.org.uk; 19 Bennett St; admission free; ⏰10.30am-6pm Mar-Oct, to 5pm Nov-Feb)

Georgian Garden
GARDENS

5 ◉ MAP P58, D5

These tiny, walled gardens feature period plants and gravel walkways. They've been carefully restored and provide an intriguing insight into what would have sat behind The Circus, one of Bath's grandest facades. (☎01225-394041; off Royal Ave; admission free; ⏰9am-7pm)

Eating

The Circus
MODERN BRITISH ££

6 ✖ MAP P58, D4

Chef Ali Golden has turned this bistro into one of Bath's destination addresses. Her taste is for British dishes with a Continental twist, à la British food writer

Bath Architecture

Bath's elegant architecture forms a tangible timeline of the city's past. From Roman through to Georgian, it's highly unusual to have so many quality buildings representing a span of so many centuries.

The building material itself is striking. Bath stone, a honey-coloured limestone, is sourced from quarries in surrounding Somerset and Wiltshire. A 'freestone', it's favoured by architects and masons because a lack of layers means it can be cut or formed into any shape.

The Roman Baths (p34) were started in 70AD and added to over the centuries that followed – the characteristic features you'll see include hypocaust stacks and arched Roman windows. These are below ground; the buildings now standing at the site were designed in the 1700s and include the grand Pump Room (p35). It's built in the neoclassical style, which echoed designs from ancient Greece and Rome.

The 18th century also brought the buildings Bath is most famous for today – the Circus and the Royal Crescent, which were designed by father and son team John Wood the Elder and John Wood the Younger. At the Circus (p60), three stories of columns feature the three orders of Greek architecture. From the ground up you'll see Doric (simple with plain tops), then Ionic (slender pillars with spiral scrolls), then Corinthian (with ornate, elaborate tops). At the curving terrace of the nearby Royal Crescent (p52) you'll see more than 100 Ionic columns.

Other notable areas for 18th-century architecture include **Gay St** just to the south, which leads into **Queen Square**, where John Wood the Elder had a home. Pulteney Bridge (p40) features three arches and – unusually – shops, while **Great Pulteney St** is a 30m-wide, 300m-long boulevard lined with Georgian terraces. The **Holburne Museum** sits at the far end.

On the outskirts of the city is Prior Park (p45), a country house that is another John Wood the Elder design, which has a rare Palladian bridge and grounds designed by Lancelot 'Capability' Brown.

The city has countless other architectural treasures – the Museum of Bath Architecture (p60) explores that rich past.

Elizabeth David: rabbit, Wiltshire lamb and West Country fish are all infused with herby flavours and rich sauces. It occupies an elegant town house near the Circus. Reservations recommended. (☏01225-466020; www.thecircusrestaurant.co.uk; 34 Brock St; mains lunch £12-15, dinner £16-23; ⊙10am-midnight Mon-Sat; 🖉)

Chequers

GASTROPUB ££

7 MAP P58, D3

A discerning crowd inhabits Chequers, a Georgian pub that's now morphed into a classy gastropub. Here the menu ranges from well-executed bar-food favourites to relative rarities such as mallard and smoked eel, and partridge with quince. (☎01225-360017; www.thechequersbar.com; 50 Rivers St; mains £14-25; ☺bar noon-11pm, food noon-2.30pm & 6-9pm)

Same Same But Different

CAFE ££

8 MAP P58, E5

In this boho hang-out for the town's trendies you can tuck into picante poached eggs for breakfast, gourmet sandwiches for lunch and afternoon cappuccino and cake. Evenings bring creative tapas – think zesty lime and coriander octopus – best sampled with a glass from the short but strong wine list. (☎01225-466856; www.same-same.co.uk; 7a Prince's Bldgs, Bartlett St; tapas £5, mains £10-12; ☺8am-6pm Mon, 8am-11pm Tue-Fri, 9am-11pm Sat, 10am-5pm Sun; 🖥)

Marlborough Tavern

GASTROPUB ££

9 MAP P58, B3

The queen of Bath's gastropubs has food that's closer to that of a fine-dining restaurant – smoked white-bean purée, and crab and ginger salad rather than bog-standard meat-and-two-veg.

Chunky wooden tables and racks of wine behind the bar give it an exclusive, classy feel. (☎01225-423731; www.marlborough-tavern.com; 35 Marlborough Bldgs; mains £13-25; ☺bar noon-11pm, food noon-2pm & 6-9.30pm)

Yen Sushi

JAPANESE ££

10 MAP P58, E4

Bath's own *kaiten* (conveyor-belt) restaurant, with colour-coded dishes of nigiri, sushi and sashimi. (www.yensushi.co.uk; 11-12 Bartlett St; sushi £5-8; ☺noon-3pm & 5.30-10.30pm Mon-Fri, noon-10.30pm Sat)

Hudson Steakhouse

STEAK £££

11 MAP P58, G2

Steak, steak and more steak is this acclaimed eatery's raison d'être.

The Bertinet Kitchen

🍽️

Many a customer of the Bertinet Bakery thinks 'I wish I could make that'. Here's your chance, a **school** (Map p58, E4; ☎01225-445531; www.thebertinetkitchen.com; 12 St Andrew's Tce; per day £170-190) offering top-quality cookery classes run by renowned French baker, Richard Bertinet. Inspirational options range from bread-making, patisserie and Viennoiserie, to knife skills, Indian street food and fresh fish. Meals will never be the same again.

Tuck into top-quality cuts from porterhouse to prime fillet, all sourced from a Staffordshire farmers' co-op. (☎01225-332323; www.hudsonsteakhouse.co.uk; 14 London St; mains £19-31; ⏰5-10.30pm Mon-Sat)

Drinking

Star

PUB

12 🚇 MAP P58, F3

Few pubs are registered relics, but the Star is just that, and it still has many of its 19th-century bar fittings. It's the brewery tap for Bath-based Abbey Ales; some ales are served in traditional jugs, and you can even ask for a pinch of snuff in the 'smaller bar'. (☎01225-425072; www.abbeyales.co.uk; 23 The Vineyards,

---

Beckford's Tower

Built as a study and library for the aristocrat William Beckford in 1827, this 120ft neoclassical **tower** (www.beckfordstower.org.uk; Lansdown Rd; adult/child £4.50/2.20; ⏰10.30am-5pm Sat & Sun Mar-Oct) is worth visiting for its eye-popping panoramic view over Bath. A spiral staircase leads to the top-floor Belvedere, while a small collection of paintings and artefacts explores Beckford's eccentric life.

The tower is about 2 miles north of the Royal Crescent along Lansdown Rd.

---

off the Paragon; ⏰noon-2.30pm & 5.30-11pm Mon-Fri, noon-midnight Sat, to 10.30pm Sun)

Corkage

WINE BAR

13 🚇 MAP P58, F3

There's a distinct air of a French bistro in this intimate, friendly wine bar where the aromas of flavour-packed dishes fill the air and regiments of bottles fill the shelves. It offers scaled-down versions of main courses (£4 to £8) and an extensive international wine list. (☎01225-422577; www.corkagebath.com; 132a Walcot St; ⏰noon-11pm Tue-Sat)

Bell

PUB

14 🚇 MAP P58, F3

Get chatting to Bath's bohemian muso crowd around the real fire at this laid-back locals' favourite. Conversation starters include the table football, bar billiards, backgammon and chess, and there's live music ranging from acoustic, country and folk to blues. (www.thebellinnbath.co.uk; 103 Walcot St; ⏰11.30am-11pm Mon-Thu, to midnight Fri & Sat, noon-10.30pm Sun; 📶)

Entertainment

Moles

LIVE MUSIC

15 ⭐ MAP P58, E5

Bath's main music venue keeps the crowds happy with a musical diet of indie, electro pop, punk, metal, club classics, DJ sets and cheesy hits. (☎01225-437537;

Beckford's Tower

www.moles.co.uk; 14 George St; ⊘5pm-3am Mon-Thu, to 4am Fri & Sat)

Shopping

Katherine Fraser   ARTS & CRAFTS

16 🔒 MAP P58, F4

The click-clack of a tabletop loom is likely to greet you as you enter this shop showcasing the skills of artisan weaver Katherine Fraser. The exquisitely worked, geometric designs in wool, silk and cotton range from covered buttons costing a few pounds to cashmere scarves for around £200. (📞01225-461341; www. katherinefraser.co.uk; 74 Walcot St; ⊘10am-5pm Mon-Sat)

Yellow Shop   VINTAGE

A treat for pre-loved clothing aficionados, the Yellow Shop is crammed with cowboy boots, chunky-knit sweaters and faded blue jeans. It's next to Katherine Fraser (see 16 🔒 Map p58, F4). (📞01225-404001; www.bathvintageclothing. co.uk; 72 Walcot St; ⊘10.30am-5.30pm Mon-Sat, noon-4pm Sun)

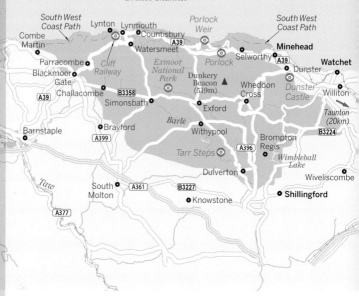

Top Sights
Exmoor National Park

Exmoor is more than a little addictive, and chances are you won't want to leave its broad, russet views. In the middle sits the higher moor, an empty, expansive, other-worldly landscape of tawny grasses and huge skies. Here, picturesque Exford makes an ideal village base. In the north, sheer, rock-strewn river valleys cut into the plateau and coal-black cliffs lurch towards the sea.

Getting There

National Express (www.nationalexpress.com) runs coaches to Taunton, Tiverton, Minehead and Barnstaple.

Nearest main-line train stations are at Taunton and Tiverton (an hour's bus ride away).

Tarr Steps

Exmoor's most famous landmark is an ancient stone clapper bridge shaded by gnarled old trees. Its huge slabs are propped up on stone columns embedded in the River Barle. Local folklore aside (which declares it was used by the Devil for sunbathing), it first pops into the historical record in the 1600s, and has had to be rebuilt after 21st-century floods. The steps are signed off the B3223 Dulverton–Simonsbath road, 5 miles northwest of Dulverton.

Dunster Castle

Rosy-hued **Dunster Castle** (NT; 📞01643-823004; www.nationaltrust.org.uk; Castle Hill; adult/child £11.60/5.80; 🕐11am-5pm Mar-Oct; 🅿) crowns a densely wooded hill. Built by the Luttrell family, the oldest sections are 13th century, while the turrets and exterior walls are 19th-century additions. Look out for Tudor furnishings, 17th-century plasterwork and a ridiculously grand staircase.

Porlock & Porlock Weir

The village of Porlock is one of the prettiest on the Exmoor coast; the huddle of thatched cottages lining its main street is framed on one side by the sea and on the other by steeply sloping hills. Winding lanes lead to the charismatic breakwater of Porlock Weir, with an arching pebble beach and striking coastal views.

Cliff Railway

Linking Lynmouth and Lynton, this extraordinary piece of **Victorian engineering** (📞01598-753486; www.cliffrailwaylynton.co.uk; The Esplanade, Lynmouth; 1-way/return adult £2.90/3.90, child £1.80/2.40; 🕐10am-5pm Feb, Mar & Oct, to 6pm Apr, May & Sep, to 7pm Jun-Aug) sees two cars, linked by a steel cable, descend and ascend the steeply sloping cliff face according to the weight of water in the cars' tanks. It's been running since 1890 and makes for an unmissable ride.

★ Top Tip

The best-known hiking routes are the Somerset & North Devon Coast Path (part of the South West Coast Path; www.southwest coastpath.org.uk), and the Exmoor section of the Two Moors Way, which starts in Lynmouth and travels south to Dartmoor and beyond.

✕ Take a Break

In Dulverton, the award-winning **Woods** (📞01598-324007; www.woodsdul verton.co.uk; 4 Bank Sq; mains £15-19; 🕐noon-2pm & 7-9.30pm) boasts menus with full-bodied flavours: confit leg of guinea fowl, slowroast lamb shoulder, and asparagus and wild-garlic risotto. Book ahead.

In Lynton, **Charlie Friday's** (📞07544 123324; www.charlie fridays.co.uk; Church Hill; snacks from £4; 🕐10am-6pm Apr-Oct, reduced hours winter; 📶🐾♿🎒) is a funky, friendly hang-out serving melt-in-your-mouth pastries, thick sarnies, and tasty nachos.

Explore ✦
Bristol City Centre

Vibrant central Bristol is the city's historic and present-day heart. It's packed with restaurants, pubs and bars, and stacked with sights ranging from unique hands-on heritage attractions to counter-culture street art. Here you'll find a broad range of places to sleep, an exciting cultural backdrop and, in the harbour area, a thriving, attractive space with a fun-loving vibe.

Head straight for the SS Great Britain (p70) and the ships and cranes of the M Shed (p74), and allow yourself at least half a day at both. While here, make sure you take in the Banksy artworks in the area – his street art is another defining characteristic of contemporary Bristol. The thought-provoking We the Curious (p80) deserves at least a few hours of your time; the old city's shops and thriving St Nicholas Market (p89), with its wealth of food stalls, are just a short walk away, while the Bristol Museum & Art Gallery (p72) is slightly further north.

Getting There & Around

🚌 The **MetroBus** (www.metrobusbristol.co.uk) M2 service runs between Bristol Temple Meads train station, the city centre, the SS *Great Britain* and Long Ashton Park and Ride.

⛴ **Bristol Ferry Boat Company** (Map p78, E4; 📞0117-927 3416; www.bristolferry.com) runs two routes, with stops including Welsh Back, the harbour near the M Shed museum, the SS *Great Britain* and Temple Meads. Bristol Packet (p83) runs harbour tours.

Bristol City Centre Map on p78

Christmas Steps street CLAUDIO DIVIZIA/SHUTTERSTOCK ©

Top Sights 📷
SS Great Britain

This is your must-visit Bristol sight – a 98m, steam-powered Victorian super ship set in a spectacular dry dock that makes it look as if she's floating in a sea of glass. You get to explore the dock, wander the deck, see the engine pounding and even climb a bit of rigging. It's evocative, hands-on history for all ages.

◎ **MAP P78, B5**

☏ 0117-926 0680

www.ssgreatbritain.org

Great Western Dock, Gas Ferry Rd

adult/child/family £16.50/9.50/45

🕓 10am-5.30pm Apr-Oct, to 4.30pm Nov-Mar

The Dry Dock

She's now more than 170 years old, and time has taken its toll on the *SS Great Britain*; her iron hull has been corroded by salt water. This is now exacerbated by moisture in the air, hence the dry dock (ingeniously capped by a glass roof), which seals the vessel in part way up her hull.

The Deck

Once on the vessel herself, you can head onto the Promenade Deck, then head for the Weather Deck to play the games passengers would have enjoyed – quoits anyone? You can also climb the rigging – **Go Aloft!** (£10; ⏱noon-5pm daily Apr-Oct, noon-3.45pm Sat & Sun Nov-Mar) sees you climbing 25m up rope ladders before edging 9m out along the yard arm. The harness and helmet makes it safer than it was in the day of the ship's designer, Isambard Kingdom Brunel.

The Steerage

The *SS Great Britain* could carry more than 600 people. And most passengers, far from enjoying the high life, were crowded into Steerage, or Third Class, for the 60-day voyage to Australia.

The Engine

The 1000-horsepower steam engine inside the vessel was the most powerful one in a ship at the time of her launch in 1843. This full-scale working model weighs 340 tons and measures three stories high.

★ **Top Tips**

○ Buy tickets online for a 5% saving on the on-the-day price.

○ Time your visit carefully; staff often get the engine running between 11am and 4pm.

○ Discovery Talks take place at 2pm – providing an insider's insight into life on board.

○ Arrive early to get a good choice of Audio Companions (aka audio guides), including one for children.

○ Like dressing up? Head to Flash! Bang! Wallop!

○ Your tickets are valid for a year – consider another trip?

○ Don't miss hearing how Victorian dockworkers 'spent a penny' at the 130-year-old *pissoir* (urinal).

✕ **Take a Break**

Drop by the waterside Dockyard Cafe (p85) for sourdough toasted sandwiches or visit Cargo (p86) for street food.

Top Sights 📷
Bristol Museum & Art Gallery

From the dinosaurs and ancient Egypt to contemporary guerrilla art, this Edwardian museum has centuries' worth of exhibits to explore. Here you'll find massive models of Jurassic beasts, ancient amulets and an iconic/iconoclastic statue created by street-art legend Banksy. Tucked in between are walls lined with old masters, a full-sized Romany caravan and a propeller-powered biplane.

⊙ MAP P78, C2

📞 0117-922 3571

www.bristolmuseums.
org.uk

Queen's Rd

admission free

🕙 10am–5pm Tue–Sun,
plus 10am–5pm Mon
school & bank holidays

Paint Pot Angel

You'll see the museum's biggest sight soon after walking in: Banksy's funerary statue of a winged woman with an upturned pot on her head – pink paint is scattered around. It's suggested that it asks us to reconsider what we might expect of museum exhibits, and reassess how we value modern art. The statue is the legacy of Banksy's 2009 takeover of the museum, when people queued for eight hours at a time to get in.

Egypt Gallery

The first door on the right leads into a beautifully lit zone packed with ancient artefacts, many focusing on beliefs, life and death. You'll find mummy cases covered in hieroglyphics, stone statues and mummified cats – killed to be an offering to the gods. Don't miss the tiny model ears (so the gods could hear your prayers) and children's toys, including miniature horses on wooden wheels.

Dinosaur Exhibits

You're about to meet some of the best-preserved dinosaurs ever found in Britain – three Scelidosaurus. It's thought the two juveniles and one adult were part of a herd that was swept out to sea and drowned. The detail is incredible – you can see their teeth, armour and even fossilised skin. You can also try to rebuild them using CGI.

Art Gallery

The walls of the 2nd floor are lined with artworks from movements such as the Italian Renaissance, Dutch Golden Age and Impressionism, along with Pre-Raphaelite and contemporary video art.

★ Top Tips

o Check the website's What's On pages for talks, tours and workshops.

o At weekends and during school holidays you can bring a packed lunch to eat in the picnic room.

o The Curiosity zone is aimed at children; there's also an under-seven's play area.

o Each floor has free wi-fi.

o Remember there's no flash photography.

✕ Take a Break

The museum's **café** (mains £6-8; ⏲10.30am-4.30pm) dishes up soup, hot specials and cakes – eat alongside an elaborate 17th-century red-brick fireplace or in the cavernous, covered atrium.

The superb sandwiches and locally roasted coffee of the Boston Tea Party (p85) are just down the road.

Top Sights 📷
M Shed

From the massive cranes and working boats and trains, to a Banksy stencil and Wallace & Gromit figurines, the M Shed busts any myths about museums being dull. And presented alongside are thoughtful displays looking at life, love and protest in Bristol through the ages, with clever juxtapositions gently prompting us to ask: what's changed?

⊙ MAP P78, E5

📞 0117-352 6600

www.bristolmuseums.org.uk

Princes Wharf

admission free

🕙 10am-5pm Tue-Sun

Boats, Trains & Cranes

The vast **Working Exhibits** alone are worth a visit. Four cargo cranes tower over the docks outside, while the 1878 curving *Fairbairn* steam crane is the oldest exhibit of its type in Britain. Riding in them provides an unforgettable view of Bristol Harbour. The *Henbury* and *Portbury* steam trains (built in 1917 and 1937, respectively) shuttle from the M Shed to the *SS Great Britain*, while the fire boat *Pyronaut* and tugboats *Mayflower* (steam) and *John King* (diesel) run regular harbour trips. The exhibits tend to be in action during summer and weekends.

Banksy's Grim Reaper

This artwork was originally stencilled on the hull of the *Thekla* nightclub ship. Depicting Death in a rowboat, the positioning right on the waterline made it look like the Grim Reaper was out for a scull. Removed amid much controversy, what you see now is actually a section of the hull, complete with stencil, rivets, silty seaweed and rust.

Wallace & Gromit

In the **Bristol People** gallery, head for the long display cases set beside the window to find two of the city's most celebrated sons. Created by local-firm Aardman Animations, the characters have now featured in four Oscar-winning films.

Slavery Displays

The Bristol People gallery also addresses Bristol's role in the slave trade and in the fight to abolish it. Chilling exhibits include a replica model of the *Brookes* slave ship, detailing the appallingly crowded conditions.

Other Displays

Visit the **Bristol Life** gallery for a witty evocation of everything from canoodling in the cinema and soccer matches, to migration and squatting.

★ Top Tips

○ Check the website to see when the Working Exhibits are in action.

○ There's free wi-fi throughout.

○ The roof terrace has great views of the waterfront and beyond.

○ Pick up an M Shed Active Alphabet leaflet for the kids.

○ There are lockers (optional) for depositing bags (£1).

○ M Shed also runs guided tours exploring the harbour's history.

✕ Take a Break

The museum's airy **M Cafe** (⊙10am-4pm Tue-Sun) serves treats such as multi-seed smoked-salmon rolls, vibrant beetroot salad, gourmet quiches and impressive cakes.

The varied food offerings of the Cargo (p86) shipping containers are tucked just behind the museum.

Walking Tour 🚶

Coffee, Culture & Craft Beer

Central Bristol is very much a local's space. Yes, there are blockbuster sights that draw the tourists, but it's also where the people who live in the city like to hang out. Vibrant, rich in culture and with an apparently endless array of places to sip coffee and beer, even on weekdays you'll find a bit of a holiday vibe.

Walk Facts

Start Small St Espresso
End Watershed
Length 1km

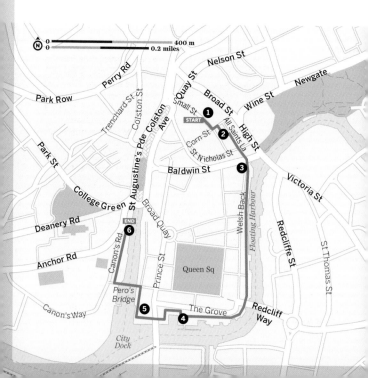

❶ Small St Espresso

Start your day at this boutique **coffee house** (www.smallstreet espresso.co.uk; 23 Small St; ⏱7.30am-4.30pm Mon-Fri, 9.30am-4.30pm Sat) that pretty much sums up Bristol's quietly cool city-centre vibe. Here you're hanging out with people who care about the art of espresso. So sit back on the settle, perch your sourdough toast on the tiny table, and try to work out whether you prefer your coffee cold-brewed or Aeropressed.

❷ St Nicholas Market

Shopping with the locals at St Nicks (p89) is an ideal way to get to grips with city life. Grab a snack from the street-food stalls in the annexe or browse the stalls inside. On Wednesdays the street outside is filled by a farmers market; Saturdays see you rummaging for bargains at the flea market.

❸ BrewDog

Time to follow the locals' lead – when you have time to spare, head for the water. All Saints Lane leads to the Floating Harbour. There the **BrewDog** (☎0117-927 9258; www. brewdog.com; 58 Baldwin St; ⏱noon-midnight Sun-Wed, to 1am Thu-Sat) pub not only provides an amiable drinking den and water-view ter-race, it also serves an impressive selection of craft beers on tap. The third-of-a-pint sampler glasses help hugely with the tasting.

❹ Mud Dock

Walking the waterside path is a popular local pastime. Heading south down Welsh Back takes you along streets once packed with traders unloading goods for the market. Today you'll see ferries, warehouses, fine restaurants and the city's famous nightclub boat *Thekla*. At **Mud Dock** (☎0117-934 9734; www.mud-dock.co.uk; 40 The Grove; ⏱10am-10pm Tue-Sat, to 4pm Mon & Sun) you can sip Bristol Beer Factory and Butcombe ales while drinking in the water views from the terrace.

❺ Arnolfini

It's worth dropping by the Front Room of the **Arnolfini** (☎0117-917 2300; www.arnolfini.org.uk; 16 Narrow Quay; admission free; ⏱11am-6pm Tue-Sun) gallery – the kind of place that's stacked with flyers and leaflets detailing local events. You can also leaf through the library of art and design books and browse what is one of the west's best specialist art bookshops.

❻ Watershed

The art-house cinema at the **Watershed** (☎0117-927 5100; www. watershed.co.uk; 1 Canon's Rd) is just a short walk on from the Arnolfini, over a pedestrian bridge and past scores of restaurants, pubs and bars. With three screens you're likely to find something to suit.

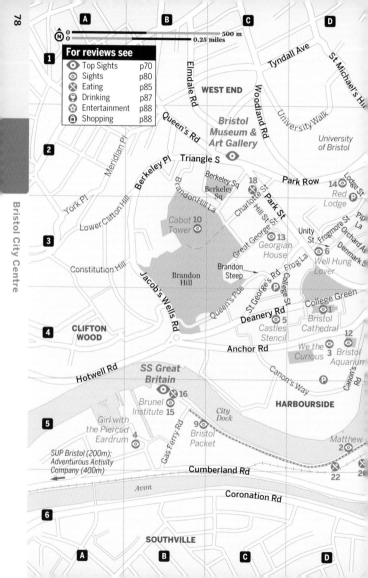

For reviews see

◉	Top Sights	p70
◎	Sights	p80
✖	Eating	p85
✗	Drinking	p87
★	Entertainment	p88
🔒	Shopping	p88

500 m
0.25 miles

WEST END

Tyndall Ave

St Michael's Hill

Elmdale Rd

Woodland Rd

University Walk

University of Bristol

Queen's Rd

Bristol Museum & Art Gallery

Meridian Pl

Triangle S

Berkeley Pl

Berkeley Sq

Berkeley Sq

18

Charlotte St

Park Row

Lodge St

14

Red Lodge

Brandon Hill La

York Pl

Park St

Hill St

Pip La

Frogmore St

Orchard A

Lower Clifton Hill

Cabot Tower 10

Great George St

13

Georgian House

Unity St

6

Denmark S

Well Hung Lover

Brandon Steep

Constitution Hill

Brandon Hill

Frog La

St George's Rd

College St

College Green

Jacob's Wells Rd

Queen's Pde

1

Bristol Cathedral

CLIFTON WOOD

Deanery Rd

5

Castles Stencil

12

Anchor Rd

We the Curious

3

Bristol Aquarium

Hotwell Rd

SS Great Britain

Canon's Way

Canon's Rd

HARBOURSIDE

Brunel Institute 15

16

City Dock

Girl with the Pierced Eardrum

4

Gas Ferry Rd

9

Bristol Packet

Matthew

2

SUP Bristol (200m);
Adventurous Activity
Company (400m)

Cumberland Rd

22

2

Avon

Coronation Rd

SOUTHVILLE

| A | B | C | D |

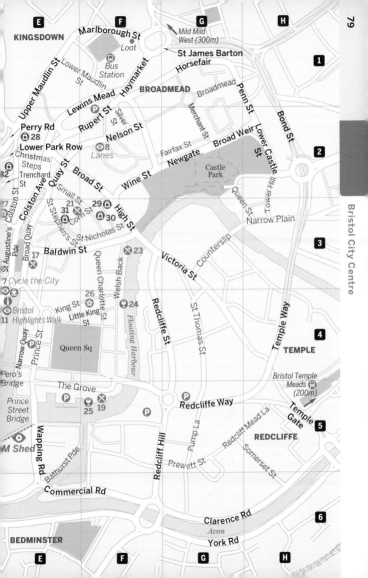

E   F   G   H

KINGSDOWN

Marlborough St

Loot

Mild Mild
West (300m)

St James Barton
Horsefair

1

Lower Maudlin St

Bus
Station

Upper Maudlin St

Lewins Mead

Haymarket

BROADMEAD

Broadmead

Penn St

Bond St

Perry Rd

28

Rupert St

Silver St

Nelson St

Merchant St

Lower Castle St

2

Lower Park Row

8

Lanes

Fairfax St

Newgate

Broad Weir

Quay St

Christmas
Steps

32

Trenchard St

Broad St

Wine St

Castle
Park

Queen St

Tower Hill

Narrow Plain

Colston Ave

Colston St

Small St

7

31 21

St Stephen's St

Corn St

29

30

High St

St Nicholas St

3

St Augustine's Pde

Broad Quay

Baldwin St

17

23

Victoria St

Counterslip

Cycle the City

7

Queen Charlotte St

Welsh Back

St Thomas St

Temple Way

Bristol
Highlights Walk

Bristol

11

26

King St

Little King St

24

Redcliffe St

4

TEMPLE

Narrow Quay

Prince St

Queen Sq

Floating Harbour

Bristol Temple
Meads
(200m)

Pero's
Bridge

The Grove

25 19

Redcliffe Way

Pump La

Temple
Gate

5

Prince
Street
Bridge

M Shed

Wapping Rd

Bathurst Pde

Redcliff Hill

Prewett St

Redcliff Mead La

Somerset St

REDCLIFFE

Commercial Rd

6

BEDMINSTER

Clarence Rd

Avon

York Rd

E   F   G   H

Sights

Bristol Cathedral
CATHEDRAL

1 ◎ MAP P78, D4

Originally founded as a 12th-century monastery church, Bristol Cathedral was heavily remodelled during the 19th century. It's one of Britain's best examples of a 'Hall Church' (meaning the nave, chapels and choir are the same height). Although the nave and west towers are Victorian, parts of the choir are medieval, and the south transept contains a rare Saxon carving of the *Harrowing of Hell,* discovered under the chapter-house floor after a 19th-century fire. (✆0117-926 4879; www.bristol-cathedral.co.uk; College Green; admission free; ⏰8am-5pm Mon-Fri, to 3.15pm Sat & Sun)

Matthew
HISTORIC SHIP

2 ◎ MAP P78, D5

The most striking thing about this replica of the vessel in which John Cabot made his landmark voyage from Bristol to Newfoundland in 1497 is its size. At 24m it seems far too small, but it would have carried a crew of around 18. Step aboard to climb below into their quarters, walk the deck and gaze up at the rigging. (✆0117-927 6868; https://matthew.co.uk; Princes Wharf; admission free; ⏰10am-4pm Tue-Sun Mar-Oct, Sat & Sun Nov-Feb)

We the Curious
MUSEUM

3 ◎ MAP P78, D4

Bristol's science museum is a playful, hands-on space where 300 'exhibits' fly the flag for curiosity, scientific collaboration and creativity. Which means you'll be meeting Aardman characters and becoming an animator for the day, discovering cosmic rays, walking through a tornado and exploring subjects ranging from anatomy to flight. There are also performances from the Live Science Team, immersive planetarium shows, and robots. Look out for After Hours – evenings designed for adults that feature games, activities and shows. (✆0117-915 1000; www.wethecurious.org; Anchor Rd; adult/child/family £15/10/40; ⏰10am-5pm Mon-Fri, to 6pm Sat & Sun)

Girl with the Pierced Eardrum
PUBLIC ART

4 ◎ MAP P78, B5

A 2014 Banksy creation that re-imagines the famous Vermeer portrait, but uses an alarm box instead of the pearl earring. It's a little hard to find – head for the

---

Blaise Castle House

This late-18th-century **house** (✆0117-903 9818; Henbury Rd; ⏰11am-4pm Thu-Sun) in the suburb of Henbury is home to a social-history museum showcasing vintage toys, costumes and an eclectic collection of Victorian ephemera. Buses 1, 3, 4 and 76 run from the city centre and stop near the museum.

clock tower of the white building outside Bristol Marina, and duck around the side.

Castles Stencil
PUBLIC ART

5 ◉ MAP P78, C4

Hidden away down the side of the Central Library, hunt out the 2011 Banksy stencil that states 'you don't need planning permission to build castles in the sky'.

Well Hung Lover
PUBLIC ART

6 ◉ MAP P78, D3

One of Banksy's best-loved pieces of street art features an apparently two-timing wife, an angry husband and a naked man dangling from a window. That it sits on the side of a sexual health clinic is surely no coincidence. (Frogmore St)

Cycle the City
CYCLING

7 ◉ MAP P78, E4

These 1½-hour bike tours of Bristol's expansive Harbourside are an ideal way to take in the city's main waterfront sights. The fee includes bike, helmet and an expert guide. The same firm also rents out bikes – if they're pre-booked (per day £16). The bike collection point, as well as the starting point for the tours, is 1 Harbourside. (☎07873 387167; www.cyclethecity.org; tours from £18)

Lanes
BOWLING

8 ◉ MAP P78, F2

The five vintage Brunswick lanes at this boutique bowling alley are all gleaming metal and polished

Banksy's *Girl with the Pierced Eardrum*

Banksy

If there's one Bristolian nearly everyone has heard of, it's Banksy (www.banksy.co.uk) – the guerrilla street artist whose distinctive stencilled style and provocative artworks have earned him world-wide notoriety.

Banksy has tried to remain anonymous but it's believed he was born in 1974 in Yate, 12 miles from Bristol, and honed his artistic skills in a local graffiti outfit. His works take a wry view of 21st-century culture – especially capitalism, consumerism and the cult of celebrity. Among his best-known pieces are the production of spoof banknotes (featuring Princess Diana's head instead of the Queen's), a series of murals on Israel's West Bank barrier (depicting people digging holes under and climbing ladders over the wall) and a painting of a caveman pushing a shopping trolley at the British Museum (which the museum promptly claimed for its permanent collection). His documentary *Exit Through the Gift Shop*, about an LA street artist, was nominated for an Oscar in 2011.

Long despised by the authorities, Banksy's artworks have become a tourist magnet. The *Well Hung Lover* (p81) depicts an angry husband, a two-timing wife, and a naked man dangling from a window. Nearby the *Castles* stencil (p81) points out 'you don't need planning permission to build castles in the sky'. The startling *Paint Pot Angel* (think pink paint meets funerary monument) resides in the Bristol Museum & Art Gallery (p72) and is a reminder of the artist's hugely popular 2009 exhibition there. **Mild Mild West** (80 Stokes Croft) features a Molotov cocktail–wielding teddy bear facing three riot police and is thought to be a comment on Bristol's edgy-yet-comfy vibe. A stencil of the Grim Reaper rowing a boat, which used to sit on the waterline of the party boat *Thekla*, is now in the city's M Shed (p74) museum. Hidden away near the SS *Great Britain, Girl with the Pierced Eardrum* (p80) is the artist's 2014 take on the famous Vermeer portrait.

The **tourist office** (Map p78, E4; ☑0333 321 0101; www.visitbristol. co.uk; E-Shed, 1 Canons Rd; ☺10am-5pm; ☎) sells a Banksy info sheet (50p), as well as the Where the Wall's colourful *Bristol Street Art Map* (£2), an informative, easy to follow trail. The excellent **Bristol Street Art Tours** (Where the Wall; ☑07748 632663; www.wherethewall. com; adult/child £9/5; ☺11am Sat & Sun) take in the main Banksy sites in a walk from the city centre to graffiti-central Stokes Croft.

wood. You'll also find a craft-beer bar and huge, crispy New York–style pizzas. The per-game rate is walk-in, if a lane is free. Alternatively, pre-book a six-person lane for an hour (£45). (📞 0117-325 1979; www.thelanesbristol.co.uk; Nelson St; per game £4-6; 🕐 noon-11pm Sun-Thu, to 2am Fri & Sat)

Bristol Packet   BOATING

9 ◎ MAP P78, B5

Bristol Packet's trips include 45-minute cruises around the harbour (adult/child £7/5, six sailings daily April to October, and on winter weekends), and weekly sailings to Beese's Tea Gardens (£14/9, April to September). Boats depart from Wapping Wharf near SS *Great Britain,* and the Watershed landing stage on the Harbourside. (📞 0117-926 8157; www.bristolpacket.co.uk; Wapping Wharf, Gas Ferry Rd)

Cabot Tower   HISTORIC BUILDING

10 ◎ MAP P78, B3

Set in the small park of Brandon Hill, this 32m ornate red-brick tower was built between 1896 and 1898 to commemorate John Cabot's pioneering voyage in search of Canada. Climbing the steep spiral staircase opens up unparalleled bird's-eye views of Bristol. (📞 0117-922 3719; Brandon Hill, near Park St; admission free; 🕐 8.15am-4.30pm)

Top Travel Tips

Central Bristol isn't huge, but you could end up walking a couple of miles end to end. A DayRider bus pass (£4.50) is a good option. Or hop on one of the services of the **Bristol Ferry Boat Company** (Map p78, E4; 📞 0117-927 3416; www.bristolferry.com). That way you get to travel and see this historic port city from the water – ideal.

Bristol Highlights Walk   WALKING

11 ◎ MAP P78, E4

Tours the old town, city centre and Harbourside, leaving from the tourist office – there's no need to book. Themed tours exploring Clifton, medieval Bristol and the history of Bristol's slave and wine trades run on request. (📞 0117-968 4638; www.bristolwalks.co.uk; adult/child £6/3; 🕐 11am Sat Mar-Sep)

Bristol Aquarium   AQUARIUM

12 ◎ MAP P78, D4

The underwater habitats you'll encounter here include a Bay of Rays, Coral Sea, Shark Tank and an Amazon River Zone. The underwater viewing tunnel adds extra appeal. Tickets are 10% cheaper online. (📞 0117-929 8929; www.bristolaquarium.co.uk; Anchor Rd, Harbourside; adult/child/family

£15/10/50; ⏰10am-4pm Mon-Fri, to 5pm Sat & Sun)

Georgian House
HISTORIC BUILDING

13 ◉ MAP P78, C3

Once the home of the wealthy slave plantation owner and sugar merchant John Pinney, this 18th-century house provides an insight into aristocratic life in Bristol during the Georgian era. It's decorated in period style, with a huge kitchen (complete with cast-iron roasting spit), book-lined library, grand drawing room, and cold-water plunge-pool in the basement. (☎0117-921 1362; www. bristolmuseums.org.uk; 7 Great George St; admission free; ⏰11am-4pm Sat-Tue Apr-Dec)

Red Lodge
HISTORIC BUILDING

14 ◉ MAP P78, D2

Built in 1590 and remodelled in 1730, this red-brick house showcases a mix of Elizabethan, Georgian and Victorian architecture and decor. The highlight is the Great Oak Room, which still features its original Tudor oak panelling, plasterwork ceiling and carved chimney piece. (☎0117-921 1360; www.bristolmuseums.org.uk; Park Row; admission free; ⏰11am-4pm Sat-Tue Apr-Dec)

Brunel Institute
LIBRARY

15 ◉ MAP P78, B5

A maritime archive housing a wealth of materials relating to engineer Isambard Kingdom Brunel, the SS *Great Britain* (p70) and Bristol's

Stand up paddleboarders on the Floating Harbour

JOE DUNCKLEY/SHUTTERSTOCK ©

Active & Outdoors Bristol

Perhaps surprisingly for one of England's largest cities, Bristol offers exciting ways to explore outdoors. Although the docks aren't used so much now for trade, the waterways remain. Here you can learn to stand up paddleboard (SUP) with **SUP Bristol** (📞0117-422 5858; www.supbristol.com; Baltic Wharf, Cumberland Rd) and paddle kayaks and canoes with the **Adventurous Activity Company** (📞01275-394558; www.adventurousactivitycompany.co.uk; Baltic Wharf, Cumberland Rd; per half day £38).

The nearby Avon Gorge offers excellent climbing. **Bloc** (📞0117-955 8508; www.blocclimbing.co.uk; Unit 2, New Gatton Rd; adult/child £10/7; ⏰10am-10pm Mon-Fri, to 6pm Sat & Sun) is one of the southwest's best bouldering walls. For cycling enthusiasts, the **Bristol & Bath Railway Path** (www.bristolbathrailwaypath.org.uk) offers 13 miles of trails.

---

naval history. To visit, bring a recent form of ID bearing your address. (📞0117-926 0680; www.ssgreatbritain. org; Great Western Dockyard; admission free; ⏰10.30am-4.30pm Tue-Fri, plus 1st & 2nd Sat per month)

Eating

Dockyard Cafe CAFE £

 16 🍴 MAP P78, B5

With a waterside terrace and big picture windows overlooking the City Dock, the Dockyard Cafe is popular with people visiting the neighbouring SS *Great Britain*. Expect bacon butties, sourdough toasted sandwiches, rich brownies and a children's menu (£2 to £5) that includes a Docker's Packed Lunch. (📞0117-926 0680; www.ssgreatbritain.org; Great Western Dockyard; mains £6-9; ⏰9.30am-6pm Easter-Oct, to 4.30pm Nov-Easter; 📶)

Pieminister FAST FOOD £

17 🍴 MAP P78, E3

In this town-centre branch of the legendary Bristol craft pie makers you'll find the usual array of quirkily named creations plus sides (think minted mushy peas), skillets (mac 'n' cheese and root veg) and beer, cider and cocktails. (📞0117-325 7616; www.pieminister. co.uk; 7 Broad Quay; pies £5.50; ⏰11.30am-9.30pm Sun-Thu, 11.30am-11pm Fri & Sat)

Boston Tea Party CAFE £

18 🍴 MAP P78, C2

First-rate sandwiches and burgers, fresh juices and locally roasted coffee are served up in style at this southwest deli chain's very first store. Brunch brings treats like chorizo hash and mushrooms on sourdough toast. (📞0117-929 8601; www.bostonteaparty.co.uk; 75 Park St;

Cargo

snacks £4-9, mains £8-10; ⏱7am-8pm Mon-Sat, 8am-7pm Sun; 📶)

Riverstation BRITISH ££

19 🔪 MAP P78, F5

Riverstation's waterside location is hard to beat, with a view over the Floating Harbour, but it's the classic food that truly shines, from confit duck leg with quince and port jus, to pan-fried turbot with squid-ink sauce. (📞0117-914 4434; www.riverstation.co.uk; The Grove; lunch 2/3 courses £14/17, dinner mains £15-18; ⏱noon-2.30pm & 6-10pm Mon-Sat, noon-3pm Sun)

Cargo STREET FOOD ££

20 🔪 MAP P78, D5

Set in scores of former shipping containers stacked two stories high on the dockside, these bijou eateries offer bites ranging from curries and burgers to fish and chips, pizza and cakes. They tend to be open daily and well into the evening, when you might have to queue. (www.wappingwharf.co.uk/cargo; Museum St; mains £6-16; ⏱times vary)

Ox STEAK ££

21 🔪 MAP P78, E3

Gorgeous, highly polished wood, glinting brass, low lighting and cool jazz ensure this sleek eatery resembles a posh Pullman dining car that's somehow been bestowed with some Pre-Raphaelite murals. The food is aimed firmly at meat eaters; expect charcuterie platters, gourmet burgers and five choices of steak cut. (📞0117-922 1001;

www.theoxbristol.com; The Basement, 43 Corn St; mains £13-27; ⏲noon-2.30pm Mon-Fri, 5-10.30pm Mon-Sat, noon-4pm Sun)

Olive Shed   BISTRO ££

22 ❌ MAP P78, D5

With tables right beside Bristol Harbour, this rustic eatery is a top spot for a waterfront lunch. It serves tapas and twists on Mediterranean food, such as pork with manzanilla glaze, fragrant rosemary cured manchego and spicy courgette, chickpea and cumin kofta. (☎0117-929 1960; www.theoliveshed.com; Princes Wharf; tapas £4-8.50, mains £12-19; ⏲noon-10pm Thu-Sat, to 5pm Sun)

Glassboat   FRENCH £££

23 ❌ MAP P78, F3

This converted river barge is an ideal spot for a romantic dinner, with candlelit tables and harbour views through a glass extension. The refined food revolves around French and Italian flavours. (☎0117-332 3971; www.glassboat.co.uk; Welsh Back; lunch 2/3 courses £12/15, dinner mains £20-32; ⏲noon-2.45pm & 5.30-9.45pm Mon-Sat, noon-4.45pm Sun)

Drinking

Apple   BAR

24 🍺 MAP P78, F4

Around 40 varieties of cider are served on this converted barge, including raspberry, strawberry and

---

Stokes Croft

In the counterculture enclave of Stokes Croft, shop shutters are smothered with swirls of spray paint and almost every surface is plastered with graffiti tags – it's one of the key stops on any street-art-aficionado's Bristol tour.

It's a gritty area with a bit of an edge. Stencils half the height of houses call for drugs to be legalised and supermarkets to be boycotted – a legacy of the riots in 2011 when, over two weekends, a chain store was targeted in what many saw as anti-capitalist protests. Today, all around you shops and cafes revel in their role as creative challengers to the status quo, and gentlemen with fine face furniture aren't really, honestly, even trying to be cool.

To explore, head up Stokes Croft road, perhaps stopping at **Treasure** (☎0117-329 2825; 100 Stokes Croft; ⏲noon-6pm Mon-Sat) for retro clothes and the **Canteen** (☎0117-923 2017; www.canteenbristol.co.uk; 80 Stokes Croft; mains £5-10; ⏲10am-midnight Mon-Thu, to 1am Fri & Sat, to 11pm Sun; 📶) for lunch and Banksy's riot-themed *Mild Mild West* mural. Then drop by **Arts House** (108 Stokes Croft; ⏲10am-11pm) for a spot of people watching and to drink in the Stokes Croft scene.

six perries (pear cider). Best enjoyed at a table set on the canalside cobbles. (☎0117-925 3500; www.apple cider.co.uk; Welsh Back; ⊙noon-midnight Mon-Sat, to 10.30pm Sun summer, 5pm-midnight Mon-Sat winter)

Thekla
CLUB

25 🚌 MAP P78, F5

Bristol's club-boat has nights for all moods: electro-punk, indie, disco and new wave, plus regular live gigs during the week. Check the website for the latest. (☎0117-929 3301; www.theklabristol.co.uk; The Grove, East Mud Dock; ⊙Thu-Sat 9.30pm-3am or 4am)

Entertainment

Bristol Old Vic
THEATRE

26 ⭐ MAP P78, F4

Established in 1766, the much-respected Old Vic is the longest continuously running theatre in the English-speaking world, and has just had a £12.5m revamp. It hosts big touring productions in its historic Georgian auditorium, plus more experimental work in its smaller studio. (☎0117-987 7877; www.bristololdvic.org.uk; 16 King St)

Colston Hall
LIVE MUSIC

27 ⭐ MAP P78, E3

Bristol's historic concert hall now has a gleaming five-floor annexe. Performers include rock, pop, folk and jazz bands, plus classical musicians and big-name comedy acts. (☎0117-203 4040; www.colston hall.org; Colston St)

Shopping

Makers
ARTS & CRAFTS

28 🔒 MAP P78, E2

The carefully curated selection of goods made by mostly local crafts-people on show here includes

---

Wallace & Gromit

One of the great success stories of English TV and cinema has been Bristol-based animator Nick Park and the production company Aardman Animations, best known for the award-winning man-and-dog duo Wallace and Gromit. This lovable pair first appeared in Park's graduation film *A Grand Day Out* (1989) and went on to star in *The Wrong Trousers* (1993), *A Close Shave* (1995) and the full-length feature *The Curse of the Were-Rabbit* (2005).

Known for their intricate plots, film homages and amazingly realistic stop-motion animation – as well as their very British sense of humour – the Wallace and Gromit films scooped Nick Park four Oscars. Other Aardman works include *Chicken Run* (2000), *Flushed Away* (2006) and *The Pirates!* (2012).

exquisite silk scarfs, fine pottery, delicate jewellery, and upcycled bathroom tiles. The owners have a simple criteria – if they don't like it, it doesn't get in. It works. (📞0117-329 0502; www.makersbristol.co.uk; 82 Colston St; ⏰10am-5.30pm Mon-Sat)

Urban Fox   VINTAGE

29 🔒 MAP P78, F3

If Bristol's hipsters have got you wanting to up your sartorial game, head here for a quality selection of pre-loved threads ranging from lumberjack shirts and hot pants to sheepskin flying jackets. (📞0117-930 0090; www.urbanfox.me; 58 Corn St; ⏰10am-6pm Mon-Sat, noon-5pm Sun)

St Nicholas Market   MARKET

30 🔒 MAP P78, F3

Quality contemporary goods sit beside heritage features in this Georgian corn exchange, making for cheery browsing among goods ranging from jewellery and cool hats to leather bags and bamboo socks. There's a farmers market outside each Wednesday (9.30am to 2.30pm), and a flea market every Saturday (9am to 4.30pm). (St Nicks Market; www.stnicholasmarketbristol.co.uk; Corn St; ⏰9.30am-5pm Mon-Sat)

Loot

One of Bristol's largest **vintage clothing shops** (Map p78, F1; 📞0117-922 0633; www.gimmetheloot.co.uk; 9 Haymarket Walk; ⏰10am-5.30pm Mon-Sat, 11am-5pm Sun) is a treasure trove of retro threads ranging from shirts and shorts to sunglasses and shoes. There's an extensive collection of artfully distressed jeans.

Stanfords   BOOKS

31 🔒 MAP P78, E3

The Bristol branch of the renowned travel bookseller is itching to fuel your wanderlust with thousands of guidebooks, explorers' accounts, atlases and maps. (📞0117-929 9966; www.stanfords.co.uk/bristol-store; 29 Corn St; ⏰9am-6pm Mon-Sat, 11am-5pm Sun)

Dig Haüshizzle   VINTAGE

32 🔒 MAP P78, E2

Vintage furniture and retro design pieces, from pine chests to apothecary jars. (📞07789 145175; www.dig-haushizzle.co.uk; 51 Colston St; ⏰10am-5pm Mon-Sat)

Explore

Clifton

Set on the edge of Bristol, Clifton is far enough away to maintain a village atmosphere, but close enough to revel in the city's cosmopolitan feel. Victorian and Georgian terraces and swaths of grassland (the Downs) make it beautiful; the Avon Gorge and Clifton Suspension Bridge add drama; and intimate eateries, hip bars and snug pubs make it inviting.

Make straight for the Clifton Suspension Bridge (p92), walk onto it from the Clifton side and cross on foot to the visitor centre on the west bank. The Clifton Observatory (p97) is worth dropping by on the east bank. The Bristol Lido (p97) will occupy half a day, but note that its pool, sauna and spa are open to nonmembers on weekday afternoons only. Clifton's other great delight is the village itself – make sure you allow at least half a day to discover its ornate Georgian and Victorian terraces and browse in the ranks of independent shops. Night-time brings an opportunity to explore the many pubs, eateries and bars.

Getting There & Around
🚌 Every 15 minutes, bus 8 shuttles from Bristol Temple Meads Train Station to Clifton, via College Green in the city centre.

Clifton Map on p96

A Clifton Village street LOU ARMOR/SHUTTERSTOCK ©

Top Sights 📷
Clifton Suspension Bridge

With a height of 76m and a span of 214m across the dramatic Avon Gorge, the Clifton Suspension Bridge is a striking sight. It was designed by Isambard Kingdom Brunel, with work starting in 1831, but riots caused a funding crisis and it was eventually opened in 1864. Today some 4 million vehicles cross it each year.

◎ MAP P96, B3

www.cliftonbridge.org.uk

Suspension Bridge Rd

Walking the Bridge

Most people walk onto the bridge from the Clifton side. Before you start to cross, look out for the remains of the landing stage to the left of the tower – this is where, before the bridge was built, workmen arrived having been transported across the gorge in a basket attached to an iron bar. As you head onto the bridge you'll notice the high fencing and signs showing the Samaritan's helpline, the result of numerous suicide attempts.

Visitor Centre Exhibits

The **Clifton Suspension Bridge Visitor Centre** (☏0117-974 4664; Suspension Bridge Rd; admission free; ◷10am-5pm) has a gallery of rejected designs and a construction timeline, which features stories of riots, decades of delays, Brunel's death, and the trappings surrounding the eventual opening. You'll also find the story of 11-year-old Mary Griffiths. In 1864 she became the first member of the public to cross the bridge, sprinting to beat the young man who was trying to race her.

Bridge Documentary

On the 1st floor of the visitor centre there's a 30-minute documentary about the bridge, featuring design sketches, interviews, construction images and letters written in the 1800s complaining about how it looked – it was, apparently, too Gothic. The highlight is the cine footage of Brunel's other iconic Bristol creation, the SS *Great Britain*, sailing under the bridge on her journey home after being salvaged in 1970.

Tours

Join one of the free, 45-minute **tours** (◷3pm Sat & Sun Easter-Oct). They set off from the Clifton Toll House on the eastern bank of the bridge; there's no need to book.

★ Top Tips

o Don't miss seeing the bridge illuminated – hundreds of bulbs are turned on each night between dusk and midnight.

o The best views of the bridge are from the path up to the Observatory, which leads uphill just behind the Clifton Toll House.

o The visitor centre sells an informative leaflet (60p) for a self-guided stroll.

o You'll see Explainers on the bridge in orange, high-visibility jackets – these volunteers are happy to answer questions.

✕ Take a Break

Head to Chapter & Holmes (p98), a cute Piaggio Ape that's parked up near the visitor centre, for fair-trade coffee and locally made cake.

Back in Clifton village, Primrose Cafe (p98) serves legendary brunches and inventive lunches.

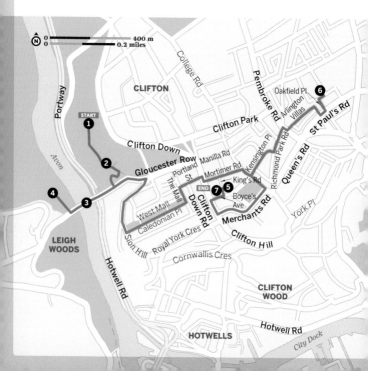

Clifton Amble

Clifton is the kind of cool neighbourhood we'd love to live in but all too often don't. Part of a vibrant city but with a village feel, here one-off shops and eateries meet welcoming pubs and chic bars. Add grassy hills, views of the Avon Gorge and a luxury lido, and you'll see why Clifton is the perfect locals' hangout.

Walk Facts

Start Clifton Downs
End Amoeba
Length 3.3km

❶ Clifton Downs

In Clifton, a walk on the Downs is a time-honoured way to start the day. This grassy strip of high ground stretches north and west of Clifton Village. If you go up the Mall, onto the footpaths and wander towards the Avon Gorge you'll spot many a local strolling and passing the time of day.

❷ Clifton Observatory

Set plum on the edge of the swooping Avon Gorge, Observatory Hill acts as a magnet for walkers. The cliff cuts away steeply here – heading into the Clifton Observatory (p97) means you can marvel at the *camera obscura* and the dizzying drop from the gorge-side viewing platform of the Giant's Cave.

❸ Clifton Suspension Bridge

It's hard to resist walking onto the Clifton Suspension Bridge (p92) – it dominates the landscape and provides a stunning vantage point from which to look onto the River Avon 76m below.

❹ Leigh Woods

Leigh Woods (NT; ☎0117-973 1645; www.nationaltrust.org.uk; admission free; ⏲24hr) is Clifton's wild heart. It packs a remarkable amount of nature into such a small space,

with ancient trees, grazing cows and cracking Avon Gorge views. There's also a network of gently sloping, well-signposted walking trails – the circular purple route (1.5m) is a popular one.

❺ Primrose Cafe

Wandering back to Clifton Village via the Mall Gardens means you can admire its grand Georgian and Victorian terraces. The Clifton Arcade is great for a spot of shopping, then stop by the Primrose cafe (p98) to brunch or lunch with the locals. This well-loved hang-out serves epic dishes; the Belgian waffles are a meal in themselves.

❻ Bristol Lido

This alfresco, naturally heated Victorian pool (p97) is utterly gorgeous. It can also be pretty exclusive – although open to swimmers on weekday afternoons, it's members only at weekends. (Unless you book a spa or dining package, but don't tell everyone.) A post-dip visit to the lido's tapas bar is a must.

❼ Amoeba

Round off the day with drinks and a bite to eat. Drop by stylish Amoeba (p99) for a superb selection of cocktails and craft beers.

Clifton

For reviews see

◈	Top Sights	p92
⊙	Sights	p97
⊗	Eating	p98
⊗	Drinking	p99
⊕	Entertainment	p100
⊕	Shopping	p100

0 — 400 m
0 — 0.2 miles

CLIFTON

CLIFTON WOOD

CLIFTON VILLAGE

LEIGH WOODS

Bristol Lido

St Paul's Rd

Oakfield Pl

Arlington Villas

Richmond Hill

Richmond Pl

Meridian Pl

Jacob's Wells Rd

Lower Clifton Hill

Clifton Hill

Constitution Hill

York Pl

Clifton Rd

Queen's Rd

Pembroke Rd

Richmond Park Rd

Pembroke Gve

Kensington Pl

Wyndham Rd

Lansdown Rd

King's Rd

Victoria Sq

Boyce's Ave

Merchants Rd

Regent St

Clifton Hill

Clifton Vale

College Rd

Clifton Park

Christchurch Rd

Manilla Rd

Mortimer Rd

Clifton Down Rd

Clifton Down Row

Gloucester Row

Clifton Down

The Downs

Clifton Observatory & Camera Obscura

Giant's Cave

Waterloo St

Portland St

The Mall

West Mall

Princess Victoria St

Victoria

Caledonia Pl

Westfield Pl

Sion Pl

Sion Hill

Royal York Cres

York Gardens

Cornwallis Cres

Hensman's Hill

Cornwallis Cres

Grain Barge (750m)

Portway

Avon

Hotwell Rd

Avon

Clifton Suspension Bridge

Leigh Woods

Sights

Clifton   AREA

1 ◉ MAP P96, C3

During the 18th and 19th centuries, wealthy Bristol merchants transformed the former spa resort of Clifton into an elegant hilltop suburb packed with impressive Georgian mansions. Some of the finest examples can be seen along **Cornwallis Crescent** and **Royal York Crescent**. These days, Clifton is still the poshest postcode in Bristol, with fancy shops and a villagey atmosphere that's far removed from the rest of the city.

Clifton Observatory & Camera Obscura   OBSERVATORY

2 ◉ MAP P96, B2

Set in a striking 18th-century windmill, Clifton Observatory features a viewing platform, a rare camera obscura and the cliff-side Giant's Cave. Together they offer incredible views of the suspension bridge, the plunging Avon Gorge and Bristol itself. (☎0117-974 1242; www.cliftonobservatory.com; Litfield Rd, Clifton Down; adult/child £2.50/1.50; ◷10am-5pm Feb-Oct, to 4pm Nov-Jan)

Giant's Cave   CAVE

3 ◉ MAP P96, B2

A natural cavern set beneath the Clifton Observatory & Camera Obscura. The cave mouth is set into the side of the cliff, offering spectacular views over the suspension bridge and Avon Gorge. (www.cliftonobservatory.com; Litfield Rd, Clifton Down; adult/child £2.50/1.50; ◷10am-5pm Feb-Oct, to 4pm Nov-Jan)

Bristol Lido   BATHHOUSE

4 ◉ MAP P96, F1

Bristol's public hot tub dates back to 1849, and, after falling into disrepair during the early 20th century, this naturally heated, 24m pool has now been restored to its steamy best – with a balmy water temperature of around 24°C. Admission includes three hours' use of the pool, sauna, steam room and outdoor hot tub. (☎0117-933 9530; www.lidobristol.com; Oakfield Pl; nonmembers £20; ◷nonmembers 1-4pm Mon-Fri)

Bristol Zoo Gardens   ZOO

5 ◉ MAP P96, D1

Highlights at the city's award-winning zoo include a family of seven western lowland gorillas (bossed by silverback Jock) and the Seal and Penguin Coast, where African penguins, eider ducks and South American fur seals lounge around. There's also a reptile and bug zone, butterfly forest, lion enclosure, monkey jungle and the **Zooropia** (adult/child £8/7) treetop adventure park. Online tickets are up to a third cheaper. To get here from the city centre, catch bus 8. (☎0117-428 5300; www.bristolzoo.org.uk; College Rd; adult/child £22/16; ◷9am-5.30pm; P)

Eating

Primrose Cafe

CAFE £

6 🌀 MAP P96, D3

The Primrose richly deserves its status as a Clifton institution, thanks to decades of serving towering homemade cakes and imaginative lunches, such as halloumi and courgette burgers, and slow-cooked pheasant. Pavement tables and a secluded roof garden add to the appeal, as do belt-busting brunches that are served impressively late (to 3pm); the eggs Benedict and Belgian waffles are legendary. (📞 0117-946 6577; www.primrosecafe.co.uk; 1 Boyce's Ave; dishes £6-10; ⏰ 9am-5pm Mon-Sat, from 9.30am Sun; 🐾)

Chapter & Holmes

CAFE £

7 🌀 MAP P96, A3

Top-notch coffee and cake served from a lovingly converted Piaggio Ape parked up near the Clifton Suspension Bridge visitor centre. (www.cliftonbridge.org.uk; Clifton Suspension Bridge; cakes £2.50; ⏰ 10am-5pm Easter-Oct)

Shop 3

BISTRO ££

8 🌀 MAP P96, D3

It's a bit like heading into a French neighbourhood bistro when you step through the door at Shop 3 to encounter the rich aromas of rustic food. The focus is firmly on local and foraged – expect delicate presentation but robust flavours from ingredients such as venison, oxtail, pheasant, artichokes and

Primrose Cafe

kale. (☎0117-382 2235; www.shop
3bistro.co.uk; 3a Regent St; mains £15-
25; ⏱6-11pm Tue-Sat)

Clifton Sausage BRITISH ££

9 ✖ MAP P96, D3

One for Brits to go all misty-eyed
over: a cool eatery that places
the much-beloved sausage on a
culinary pedestal. The varieties
on offer here include Gloucester
pork, Cotswold lamb, and beef and
Butcombe ale – all come with a
dollop of gourmet mash. (☎0117-
973 1192; www.cliftonsausage.co.uk;
7 Portland St; mains £11-17; ⏱noon-
4pm & 6-10pm Mon-Sat, 10am-4pm &
6-9pm Sun)

Thali Café INDIAN ££

10 ✖ MAP P96, D3

At Thali, something of the makeshift exuberance of Indian street
food comes to Clifton's hills.
Richly flavoured dishes infused
with spices include the epony-
mous thalis (multicourse meals),
showcasing different curry styles.
To drink? Perhaps a Jaipur IPA,
dry gin with homemade tonic, or
cup of chai. (☎0117-974 3793; www.
thethalicafe.co.uk; 1 Regent St; meals
£9-12; ⏱5-10pm Mon-Fri, from noon
Sat & Sun)

Fishers SEAFOOD ££

11 ✖ MAP P96, D3

Bristol's top choice for fish dishes
rustles up everything from garlicky
pan-fried bream with pesto, to suc-
culent grilled whole lobster. The

Ashton Court Estate

This huge **estate** (www.
ashtoncourtestate.com; Long
Ashton; parking per day £1.20;
⏱8am-dusk) around 2 miles
west of the city centre is
Bristol's 'green lung', with
850 sprawling acres of oak
woodland, trails and public
park. It hosts many of Bristol's
key events, including balloon
and kite festivals. There are
also 4.5 miles of bike trails,
two 18-hole golf courses, three
orienteering courses and a
miniature railway.

 If you're really lucky, you
might even spot a roe or fallow
deer.

hot shellfish platter (£46 for two
people) is memorable. The simple
setting, with its whitewashed walls,
ship's lanterns and nautical knick-
knacks, adds to the maritime
vibe. (☎0117-974 7044; www.fishers
-restaurant.com; 35 Princess Victoria
St; mains £14-25; ⏱5.30-10pm Mon,
noon-3pm & 5.30-10pm Tue-Sun)

Drinking

Amoeba CRAFT BEER

12 MAP P96, D3

Sixty-five craft beers, 60 cocktails
(£8 to £9) and a hundred-and-
something (who's counting?)
spirits draw style-conscious
drinkers to this chilled-out wine
bar, where patrons sit on bench

seats smothered in cushions and nibble on platters of charcoal crackers and artisan cheese (£8). (📞 0117-946 6461; www.amoeba clifton.co.uk; 10 Kings Rd; ⏰ 4pm-midnight Mon-Thu, 1pm-1am Fri & Sat, 1pm-midnight Sun)

Coronation Tap PUB

13 🚇 MAP P96, C3

As they love to tell you at the Cori, the pub is older than the Clifton Suspension Bridge. These days it's a lively spot beloved by students, with an impressive range of ciders on tap, including the exclusive tipple Exhibition – it goes down rather easily considering it's a hefty 8.4%. Luckily it's only sold in half pints. (📞 0117-973 9617; www.thecoronationtap.com; 8 Sion Pl; ⏰ 5.30-11pm Mon-Fri, from 7pm Sat & Sun)

Grain Barge

This lovingly converted 1930s **cargo vessel** (📞 0117-929 9347; www.grainbarge.com; Mardyke Wharf, Hotwell Rd; ⏰ noon-11pm Sun-Wed, to 11.30pm Thu-Sat) used to transport barley and wheat. Fittingly it's now used by the Bristol Beer Factory to showcase its craft ales. The beer terrace on the barge's roof is a cool spot to watch river traffic drift by.

There's live music on Thursday nights (from 8pm).

Albion PUB

14 🚇 MAP P96, D3

Cliftonites make a beeline for this village local for a post-work pint, drawn by the mini armchairs, log burner, a beer terrace framed by fairy lights and Bath Ales on tap. (www.thealbionclifton.co.uk; Boyce's Ave; ⏰ 9am-midnight Mon-Sat, to 11pm Sun)

Entertainment

Bristol Fringe LIVE MUSIC

15 ⭐ MAP P96, D3

There's live music most nights of the week at the Fringe, a convivial low-key local that draws a discerning crowd of often older music fans. It's particularly famous for its jazz sessions on Wednesday nights from 8pm. (📞 0117-330 0900; www.thebristolfringe.co.uk; 32 Princess Victoria St; ⏰ 4pm-midnight Mon-Fri, from 3pm Sat & Sun)

Shopping

Jemima Rose VINTAGE

16 🔒 MAP P96, D3

A cut above many a retro shop in terms of quality, at Jemima Rose you'll find high-class once-loved and designer items, ranging from knee-high boots and Burberry trench coats to 1930s beaded flapper gowns. (📞 0781-278 1176; www.jemimarose.co.uk; 4 Clifton Arcade; ⏰ 10am-5.30pm Mon-Sat, 11am-4pm Sun)

Grain Barge on the waterfront

Dustbowl
VINTAGE

Time to channel your inner James Dean. Beloved by Clifton's wannabe beatniks, this shop, next to Jemima Rose (see **16** 🔒 Map p96, D3), is bursting with top-notch mid-20th-century American menswear – think work boots, checked shirts, mountain smocks, varsity jackets and, of course, jeans. (📞 0117-973 1091; www.dustbowlvintage.com; 6 Clifton Arcade; 🕙 noon-5pm Wed-Sat, to 3pm Sun)

Papersmiths
STATIONERY

17 🔒 MAP P96, D3

This is probably the best stationery shop in Bristol. All stock – notebooks of many purposes and sizes, pencils of countless lead widths and colours, pens to smarten even the scrawliest handwriting, over 100 niche magazines – is curated with beauty, purpose and simplicity in mind. (📞 0117-329 6347; www.papersmiths. co.uk; 6a Boyce's Ave; 🕙 10am-6pm Mon-Sat, 11am-5pm Sun)

Top Sights 📷
Isle of Wight

*For decades this slab of rock anchored off
Portsmouth was a magnet for family holidays,
and seaside kitsch survives in bucket- and spade-
fulls. But there's much more: a long-running
music festival draws partygoers, just-caught seafood is served in kooky fishers' cafes, cool camp-
ing rules and there's a mild climate, outdoorsy
activities and a 25-mile shore lined with beaches,
dramatic white cliffs and tranquil sand dunes.*

www.visitisleofwight.co.uk

Osborne House

Osborne House (EH; 01983-200022; www.english-heritage.org.uk; York Ave; adult/child £17.20/10; 10am-6pm Apr-Sep, to 5pm Oct, to 4pm Sat & Sun Nov-Mar; P) in the hilly Georgian harbour town of Cowes is pure Victorian pomp. It was built in the 1840s at the behest of Queen Victoria. Extravagant rooms include the opulent Royal Apartments and Durbar Room.

Brading Roman Villa

The exquisitely preserved mosaics (including a famous cockerel-headed man) at this **villa** (01983-406223; www.bradingromanvilla.org.uk; Morton Old Rd; adult/child £9.50/4.75; 10am-5pm) ruin on the outskirts of the town of Brading in the east of Wight make this one of the finest Romano-British sites in the UK.

Needles Old & New Battery

Wight's westerly corner is where the island really comes into its own. Sheer white cliffs rear from a surging sea as the stunning coastline peels west to Alum Bay and the most famous chunks of chalk in the region: the Needles. These jagged rocks rise, shardlike, out of the sea, like the backbone of a prehistoric sea monster. The Victorian **fort** (NT; 01983-754772; www.nationaltrust.org.uk; The Needles; adult/child £6.80/3.40; 11am-4pm mid-Mar–Oct) complex at Wight's western tip is home to two gun emplacements where engrossing displays reveal how the site was established in 1862, served in two world wars and then became a secret Cold War rocket-testing base.

Festivals & Events

The **Isle of Wight Music Festival** (mid-Jun) kicked off in 1968, when an estimated 200,000 hippies came to see The Who, Joni Mitchell and Jimi Hendrix' last performance. Generations on, its gatherings are still some of England's top musical events. **Cowes Week** (www.aamcowesweek.co.uk; early Aug), first held in 1826, is one of the biggest sailing regattas in the world.

★ **Getting There & Away**

Hovertravel (01983-717700; www.hovertravel.co.uk; Quay Rd, Ryde) runs hovercraft from Southsea and Ryde. **Red Funnel** (02380-248500; www.redfunnel.co.uk) runs ferries from Southampton. **Wightlink Ferries** (0333 999 7333; www.wightlink.co.uk) runs boats from Portsmouth and Lymington.

✖ **Take a Break**

In Ryde, **Black Sheep** (01983-811006; www.theblacksheepbar.co.uk; 53 Union St; mains £8-12; noon-3pm Mon-Fri, 6-9pm Wed-Fri, 10am-5pm Sat, 10am-3pm Sun) offers homemade burgers, tasty sandwiches and steaming bowls of mussels.

Ventnor's **Ale & Oyster** (01983-857025; www.thealeandoyster.co.uk; The Esplanade; mains £22-25; noon-2pm & 6-9pm Wed-Sun) is a top-notch bistro with refined dishes and bay views.

Explore ◎
Wiltshire

Wiltshire's verdant landscape is littered with more mysterious stone circles, processional avenues and ancient barrows than anywhere else in Britain. Take prehistoric Stonehenge and the atmospheric stone ring at Avebury and add 800-year-old Salisbury cathedral, the stately homes at Stourhead and Longleat and the impossibly pretty village of Lacock, and you've a county crammed with English charm.

After breakfast in Salisbury, explore Salisbury Cathedral (p107), but aim to be on a tour (p107; book up front). Visit the Chapter House to admire the copy of the Magna Carta (p107) and savour the historic charms of the medieval Cathedral Close (p107). For lunch, enjoy fine British cuisine at Charter 1227 (p110) by historic Market Square (p108). After lunch, drive to Stonehenge (p122) and its impressive visitor centre, via the grassy ramparts of Old Sarum (p108). Round off your day by continuing north to Avebury to see the world's largest stone circle (p113) and downing a pint at the world's only pub within a stone circle, the Red Lion (p115).

Getting There & Around

🚆 Trains run from London Waterloo to Salisbury (£23, 1½ hours, at least hourly), and to Exeter and Plymouth.

🚌 First (www.firstgroup.com) serves west Wiltshire; Salisbury Reds (www.salisburyreds.co.uk) covers Salisbury and many rural areas; and Stagecoach (www.stagecoachbus.com) runs around Swindon and Salisbury.

Wiltshire Map on p116

Gate to Cathedral Close (p107), Salisbury NUSSAR/SHUTTERSTOCK ©

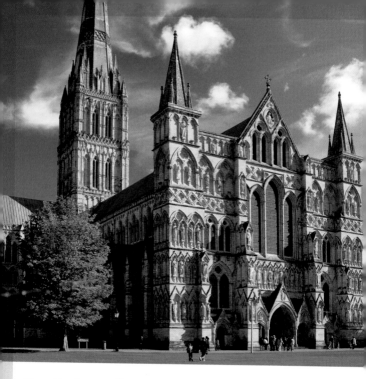

Top Sights 📷
Salisbury

Centred on a majestic cathedral that's topped by the tallest spire in England, Salisbury makes an appealing Wiltshire base. It's been an important provincial city for more than a thousand years, and its streets form an architectural timeline ranging from medieval walls and half-timbered Tudor town houses to Georgian mansions and Victorian villas.

◎ MAP P116, E6

https://www.visitwiltshire.co.uk/salisbury

Salisbury's Big Hitters

England is endowed with countless stunning churches, but few can hold a candle to the grandeur and sheer spectacle of 13th-century **Salisbury Cathedral** (☏01722-555120; www. salisburycathedral.org.uk; The Close; requested donation adult/child £7.50/3; ☻9am-5pm Mon-Sat, noon-4pm Sun), pictured left. This early English Gothic–style structure has an elaborate exterior decorated with pointed arches and flying buttresses, and a sombre, austere interior designed to keep its congregation suitably pious. Its statuary and tombs are outstanding.

The best way to explore the spectacular architecture of Salisbury Cathedral is on a 90-minute **Salisbury Cathedral Tower Tour** (adult/child £13.50/8.50; ☻2-5 tours daily, May-Sep), which sees you climbing 332 vertigo-inducing steps to the base of the spire for jaw-dropping views across the city and the surrounding countryside. They only take 12 people on each tour; booking is essential.

The **Magna Carta** (☻9.30am-5pm Mon-Sat, noon-4pm Sun Apr-Oct, 9.30am-4.30pm Mon-Sat, noon-3.45pm Sun Nov-Mar) on display in the cathedral's 13th-century **Chapter House** is one of only four surviving original copies. A historic agreement made in 1215 between King John and his barons, it acknowledged the fundamental principle that the monarch was not above the law. It's a still-powerful document, beautifully written and remarkably well preserved. It's displayed in an interactive exhibit.

Salisbury's medieval **Cathedral Close**, a hushed enclave surrounded by beautiful houses, has an other-worldly feel. Many of the buildings date from the 13th century, although the area was heavily restored during an 18th-century clean up by James Wyatt. The close is encircled by a sturdy outer wall, constructed in 1333; the stout gates leading into the complex are still locked every night. Also at Cathedral Close you'll find the **Bishop's Palace**, parts of

★ Top Tips

o A good source of local information is the **Salisbury Tourist Office** (☏01722-342860; www.visitsalisbury.co.uk; Fish Row; ☻9am-5pm Mon-Fri, 10am-4pm Sat, 10am-2pm Sun; 🛜)

o **Salisbury Guides** (☏07873-212941; www.salisburycityguides.co.uk; adult/child £6/3; ☻11am daily Apr-Oct, 11am Sat & Sun Nov-Mar) offers 90-minute guided tours that leave from the tourist office.

which date back to 1220. It's now the Cathedral School.

The **College of Matrons**, distinguished by an ornate facade and elaborate crest, is also at Cathedral Close. It was founded in 1682 for the widows and unmarried daughters of clergymen, and sits just inside narrow **High St Gate**.

The hugely important archaeological finds at the **Salisbury Museum** (☎ 01722-332151; www.salisburymuseum.org.uk; 65 The Close; adult/child £8/4; ⏰ 10am-5pm Mon-Sat year-round, & noon-5pm Sun Jun-Sep) include the Stonehenge Archer, the bones of a man found in the ditch near the stone circle – one of the arrows found alongside probably killed him. With gold coins dating from 100 BC and a Bronze Age gold necklace, it's a powerful introduction to Wiltshire's prehistory.

Salisbury's Stately Architecture

Magnificent plasterwork ceilings, exceptional period furnishings and a sweeping carved staircase grace the fine Queen Anne building that is **Mompesson House** (NT; ☎ 01722-335659; www.nationaltrust.org.uk; The Close; adult/child £6.50/3.40; ⏰ 11am-5pm mid-Mar–Oct, 11am-3.30pm Thu-Sun Nov & Dec), which dates back to 1701. It was the perfect location for the 1995 film Sense and Sensibility.

On a grass-covered hill, 2 miles north of Salisbury, you'll find the huge ramparts of **Old Sarum** (EH; ☎ 01722-335398; www.english-heritage.org.uk; Castle Rd; adult/child £5.20/3.10; ⏰ 10am-6pm Apr-Sep, to 5pm Oct, to 4pm Nov-Mar; P).

You can wander the grassy ramparts, see the original cathedral's stone foundations, and look across the Wiltshire countryside to the spire of the present Salisbury Cathedral. Medieval tournaments, jousts, open-air plays and mock battles are held on selected days. Bus X5 runs hourly from Salisbury to Old Sarum (£2.30), Monday to Saturday. It's also a stop on the Stonehenge Tour bus.

In the centre of town, markets were first held in Salisbury's **Market Square** in 1219, and the square still bustles with traders every Tuesday and Saturday (from 8am to 4pm), when you can pick up anything from fresh fish to discount watches. The narrow lanes surrounding the square reveal their medieval specialities: Oatmeal Row, Fish Row and Silver St.

Here you'll also find the **Poultry Cross**, which dates from the 15th century, the last of four crosses that once stood on the square.

The stately **St Thomas's Church** (☎ 01722-322537; www.stthomassalisbury.co.uk; Minster St; admission free; ⏰ 9am-5pm Mon-Sat, noon-5pm Sun) was built for cathedral workmen in 1219 and named after Thomas Becket. Its most famous feature is the amazing doom painting above the chancel arch, painted in 1475, which depicts Christ on the Day of Judgement, sitting astride a rainbow flanked by visions of Heaven and Hell.

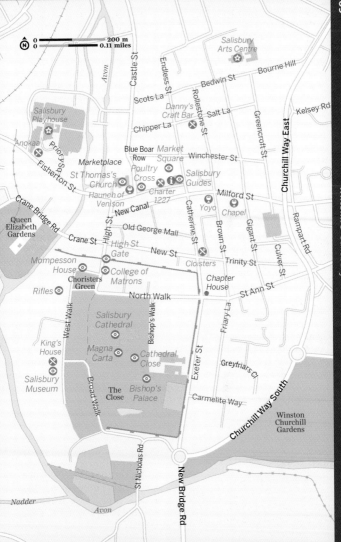

N

0 ——————— 200 m
0 ——————— 0.11 miles

Salisbury Arts Centre

Castle St
Endless St
Bedwin St
Bourne Hill
Avon
Scots La
Rollestone St
Kelsey Rd
Danny's Craft Bar
Salt La
Greencroft St
Chipper La
Churchill Way East
Salisbury Playhouse
Priory Sq
Blue Boar Row
Market Square
Winchester St
Anokaa
Fisherton St
Marketplace
Poultry Cross
Salisbury Guides
Milford St
St Thomas's Church
Charter 1227
Yoyo
Chapel
Rampart Rd
Haunch of Venison
New Canal
Catherine St
Brown St
Gigant St
Crane Bridge Rd
Old George Mall
Culver St
Queen Elizabeth Gardens
Crane St
High St Gate
New St
Trinity St
High St
Cloisters
Mompesson House
Choristers Green
College of Matrons
North Walk
Chapter House
St Ann St
Rifles
West Walk
Salisbury Cathedral
Bishop's Walk
Friary La
Exeter St
Greyfriars Cl
King's House
Magna Carta
Cathedral Close
Salisbury Museum
Broad Walk
The Close
Bishop's Palace
Carmelite Way
Winston Churchill Gardens
Churchill Way South
St Nicholas Rd
New Bridge Rd
Nadder
Avon

Nearby: Woodhenge

Woodhenge (EH; ☎ 0370 333 1181; www.english-heritage.org.uk; Countess Rd; admission free; ☺ dawn-dusk) is a series of six concentric rings that would once have been staked out by wooden posts (today, concrete markers do the job), and may have supported a building. Excavations in the 1970s revealed the skeleton of a child with a cloven skull buried near the centre. Woodhenge is some 1.5 miles east of Stonehenge, near Amesbury.

Salisbury Eats

A cafe just made for sightseeing: attached to Salisbury Museum, **King's House** (☎ 01722-332151; www.salisburymuseum.org.uk; 65 The Close; snacks from £4; ☺ 11am-3pm Tue-Sat) is a perfect spot to refuel on well-filled sandwiches and decadent cakes. It also boasts fine views of the soaring spire of neighbouring Salisbury Cathedral from the flower-framed garden.

Ingredients that speak of classic English dishes have a firm foothold at **Charter 1227** (☎ 01722-333118; www.charter1227.co.uk; 6 Ox Row, Market Pl; mains £15-30; ☺ noon-2.30pm & 6-9.30pm Tue-Sat). Feast on duck confit, beef fillet or roast lamb; the cooking and presentation are assured. Canny locals eat at lunchtime or between 6pm and 7pm Tuesday to Thursday, when mains are capped at £10 to £15.

Danny's Craft Bar (☎ 01722-504416; www.dannyscraftbar.co.uk; 2 Salt Lane; burgers £7-13; ☺ 5-9pm Mon-Thu, noon-9pm Fri, 9am-9pm Sat,

Woodhenge

Salisbury by Night

To unwind after taking in the sights, Salisbury has a few options:

Yoyo (www.yoyobar.co.uk; 6 Milford St; cocktails from £7; ☉8pm-3am Fri & Sat, to 1am Wed, to 2am Thu) Unashamedly chasing a quirky, retro-chic vibe, Yoyo is the spot to indulge in nostalgic board games and cool cocktails. The mojito list alone is six strong. Or opt to have the mixologist's masterpiece served on a tray with biscuits – dubbed Tea for 2.

Haunch of Venison (www.haunchpub.co.uk; 1 Minster St; ☉11am-11pm Mon-Sat, to 6pm Sun) Featuring wood-panelled snugs, spiral staircases and crooked ceilings, this 14th-century drinking den is packed with atmosphere – and ghosts. One is a cheating whist player whose hand was severed in a game – look out for his mummified bones on display inside.

Chapel (www.chapelnightclub.co.uk; 34 Milford St; ☉10pm-3am Thu-Sat) Buzzing three-room club with adjoining bar where the DJ sets range from funk to '90s hip hop and chart 'n' cheese.

Salisbury Playhouse (Wiltshire Creative; ☎01722-320333; www.salisbury playhouse.com; Malthouse Lane) An acclaimed producing theatre that also hosts top touring shows and musicals.

Salisbury Arts Centre (Wiltshire Creative; ☎01722-320333; www.salisbury artscentre.co.uk; Bedwin St) An innovative venue showcasing cutting-edge theatre, indie films, dance and live gigs.

9am-5pm Sun; 🛜📶) is a hip hangout with plenty on offer: breakfast on chorizo and avocado tortilla, syrup-drenched pancakes or cheesy beans. Come evening, craft beer and cocktails usher in towering burgers and hand-cut fries. It's Tex-Mex, fun and cool.

The pink-neon sign for **Anokaa** (☎01722-414142; www.anokaa.com; 60 Fisherton St; mains £14-19; ☉noon-2pm & 5.30-11pm; 📶) signals what's in store here: a modern, multi-layered take on high-class Indian cuisine. The spice and flavour combos make the ingredients sing, the meat-free menu makes vegetarians gleeful, and the lunchtime buffet (£9) makes everyone smile.

For decent pub grub, there's **Cloisters** (☎01722-338102; 83 Catherine St; mains from £8; ☉noon-2pm & 6-8pm), a 300-year-old pub in the heart of town.

Top Sights 📷
Avebury

Avebury may lack the dramatic trilithons of its sister site Stonehenge, across Salisbury Plain, but it's just as rewarding to visit. It's bigger and older, and a large section of the village is inside the stones – footpaths wind around them, allowing you to really soak up the extraordinary atmosphere. Avebury also boasts an encircling landscape that's rich in prehistoric sites and a manor house where restored rooms span five completely different eras.

◉ MAP P116, E2

Avebury's Attractions

With a diameter of 348m, **Avebury Stone Circle** (NT; ☎01672-539250; www.nationaltrust.org.uk; admission free; ⏱24hr; P), pictured left, is the largest in the world. It's also one of the oldest, dating from 2500 to 2200 BC. Today, more than 30 stones are in place; pillars show where missing stones would have been. Wandering between them emphasises the site's sheer scale, evidenced also by the massive bank and ditch that line the circle; the quieter northwest sector is particularly atmospheric. National Trust–run guided walks (£3) are held on most days.

Modern roads into Avebury neatly dissect the circle into four sectors. Starting at High St near the **Henge Shop** (☎01672-539229; www.hengeshop.com; High St; ⏱9.30am-5pm) and walking around the circle in an anticlockwise direction, you'll encounter 11 standing stones in the southwest sector. They include the **Barber Surgeon Stone**, named after the skeleton of a man found under it – the equipment buried with him suggests he was a barber-cum-surgeon.

The southeast sector starts with huge **portal stones** marking the entry to the circle from West Kennet Ave. The **southern inner circle** stood in this sector and within this ring was the **obelisk** and a group of stones known as the **Z Feature**. Just outside this smaller circle, only the base of the **Ring Stone** survives.

In the **northern inner circle** in the northeast sector, three sarsens remain of what would have been a rectangular **cove**. The northwest sector has the most complete collection of standing stones, including the massive 65-tonne **Swindon Stone**, one of the few never to have been toppled.

South of Avebury, rising abruptly from the fields, 40m-high **Silbury Hill** (EH; www.english-heritage.org.uk; admission free; P) is the largest

★ Getting There & Away

Bus 49 runs hourly to Swindon (£3, 30 minutes) and Devizes (£3, 15 minutes). There are six services on Sunday.

✖ Take a Break

Both Avebury's National Trust site and the Red Lion pub (p115) offer food. Another option is to pack a picnic and snack on the grass inside the stone circle itself.

artificial earthwork in Europe, comparable in height and volume to the Egyptian pyramids. It was built in stages from around 2500 BC, but the precise reason for its construction remains unclear. Direct access to the hill isn't allowed, but you can view it from nearby footpaths and a layby on the A4.

A footpath leads from Avebury Stone Circle 2 miles across the fields (via Silbury Hill) to **West Kennet Long Barrow** (EH; ☎ 0370 333 1181; www.english-heritage.org.uk; admission free; ☉ dawn-dusk), England's finest burial mound, and dating from around 3500 BC. Its entrance is guarded by huge sarsens and its roof is made out of gigantic overlapping capstones. About 50 skeletons were found when it was excavated; finds are

on display at the Wiltshire Heritage Museum in Devizes. The barrow is a half-mile walk across fields from the parking layby.

East of the stone circle is 16th-century **Avebury Manor** (NT; ☎ 01672-539250; www.nationaltrust.org.uk; adult/child £10.50/5.25; ☉ 11am-4pm mid-Feb–Mar, to 5pm Apr-Oct, to 4pm Thu-Sun Nov & Dec), where the mother of all makeovers used original techniques and materials to recreate interiors spanning five periods. Being hands-on is encouraged here, so now you can sit on beds, play billiards and listen to the gramophone in rooms that range from Tudor through the Georgian era to the 1930s. Visits are by timed ticket only, so it's best to arrive early to bag a slot.

West Kennet Long Barrow

Ritual Landscape

Avebury is surrounded by a network of ancient monuments, including Silbury Hill (p113) and West Kennet Long Barrow. To the south of the village, **West Kennet Avenue** stretched out for 1.5 miles, lined by 100 pairs of stones. It linked the Avebury circle with a site called the **Sanctuary**. Postholes indicate that a wooden building surrounded by a stone circle once stood at the Sanctuary, although no one knows quite what the site was for.

Nearby the manor is stout **St James Church** (admission free; ⊙9am-5pm) with Saxon and Norman features.

If walking is your thing, the 87-mile **Ridgeway National Trail** (www.nationaltrail.co.uk/ridgeway) starts near Avebury village and runs eastwards across Fyfield Down, where many of the sarsen stones at Avebury (and Stonehenge) were collected.

Avebury Refreshments

The elegant **Avebury Manor Tea Room** (www.nationaltrust.org. uk; snacks from £4; ⊙noon-5pm Easter-Oct), in the library of historic Avebury Manor, sets the scene for soups, jacket potatoes, brownies and a classic afternoon tea: fresh-baked scones, tiered cake stands and loose-leaf tea.

On the fringes of Avebury's Stone Circle sits the aptly named **Circles** (www.nationaltrust.org.uk; mains from £7; ⊙10am-5.30pm Apr-Oct, to 4pm Nov-Mar; ☑), a veggie and wholefoods cafe that serves homemade quiches and cakes, chunky sandwiches and afternoon teas.

If it's a pint you're after, in Avebury that means downing a drink at **Red Lion** (www.oldenglishinns. co.uk; High St; ⊙11am-11pm), the only pub in the world inside a stone circle. The best table is the Well Seat, where the glass tabletop covers a 26m-deep, 17th-century well – believed to be the last resting place of at least one unfortunate villager.

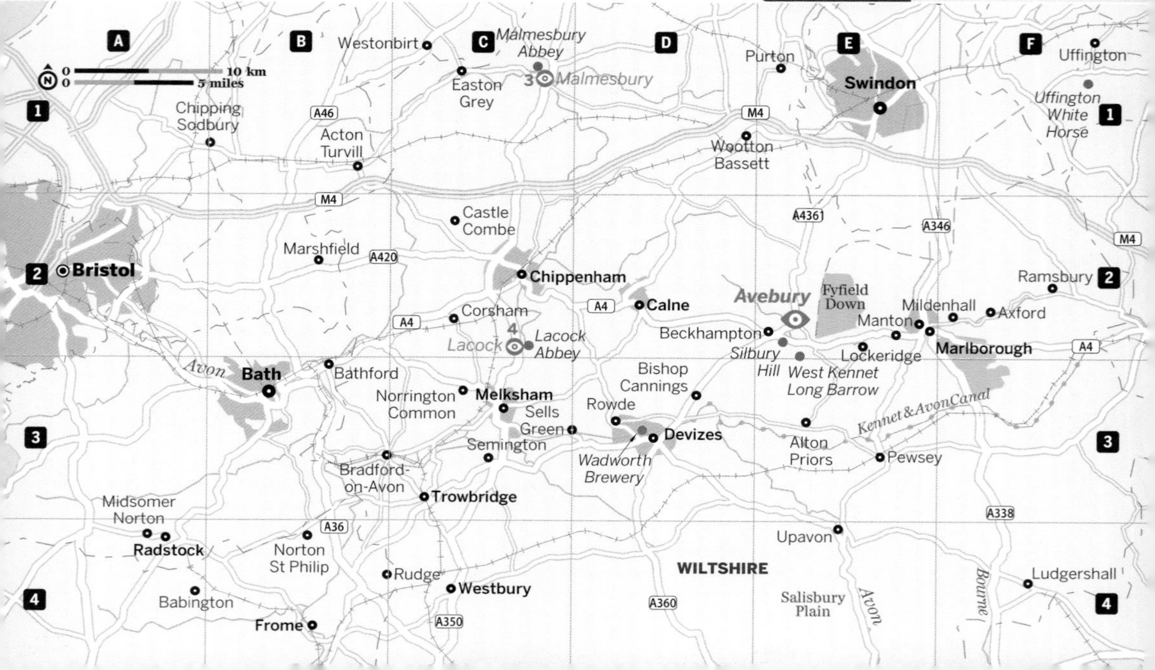
A
B
C
D
E
F
1
2
3
4
0 10 km
0 5 miles
Westonbirt
Malmesbury Abbey
3 Malmesbury
Easton Grey
Purton
Swindon
Uffington
Uffington White Horse
Chipping Sodbury
A46
Acton Turvill
M4
Wootton Bassett
Castle Combe
Marshfield
A420
A4361
A346
Bristol
Chippenham
Calne
A4
Avebury
Fyfield Down
Mildenhall
Axford
Ramsbury
Manton
Marlborough
Corsham
4 Lacock
Lacock Abbey
Beckhampton
Silbury Hill
West Kennet Long Barrow
Lockeridge
Avon
Bath
Bathford
Norrington Common
Melksham
Sells Green
Bishop Cannings
Rowde
Devizes
Kennet & Avon Canal
Alton Priors
Pewsey
Semington
Wadworth Brewery
Bradford-on-Avon
Trowbridge
Midsomer Norton
Radstock
A36
Norton St Philip
Upavon
A338
Rudge
Westbury
WILTSHIRE
Salisbury Plain
Bourne
Ludgershall
Babington
Frome
A350
A360

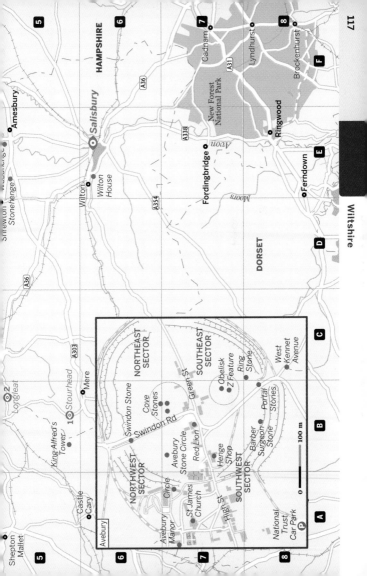

HAMPSHIRE

DORSET

Amesbury

Stonehenge

Shrewton

Salisbury

Wilton
Wilton House

A36

A303

Mere

Stourhead

Longleat

King Alfred's Tower

Shepton Mallet

Castle Cary

A36

A354

A338

Fordingbridge

Avon

Moors

Ferndown

Ringwood

New Forest National Park

A31

Cadnam

Lyndhurst

Brockenhurst

Avebury

NORTHWEST SECTOR

NORTHEAST SECTOR

SOUTHEAST SECTOR

SOUTHWEST SECTOR

Swindon Stone

Cove Stones

Swindon Rd

Green St

Obelisk

Z Feature

Ring Stone

West Kennet Avenue

Avebury Stone Circle

Red Lion

Henge Shop

Barber Surgeon Stone

Portal Stones

Avebury Manor

Circle

St James Church

High St

National Trust Car Park

0   100 m

Stourhead

1 MAP P116, B5

Overflowing with vistas, temples and follies, **Stourhead** (NT; 📞01747-841152; www.nationaltrust.org.uk; Mere; adult/child £16.60/8.30; 🕐11am-4.30pm early Mar–early Nov, to 3.30pm mid-Nov–late Dec; P) is landscape gardening at its finest. The Palladian house has some fine Chippendale furniture and paintings by Claude and Gaspard Poussin, but it's a sideshow to the magnificent 18th-century gardens (open 9am to 5pm), which spread out across the valley. Here you'll also find **King Alfred's Tower** (adult/child £4.40/2.20; 🕐noon-4pm Sat & Sun Mar–Oct), a 50m-high folly with wonderful views. Stour-head is off the B3092, 8 miles south of Frome.

Longleat

2 MAP P116, B5

Half ancestral mansion, half wildlife park, **Longleat** (📞01985-844400; www.longleat.co.uk; near Warminster; all-inclusive ticket adult/child £35/26, house & grounds £19/14; 🕐10am-5pm Feb–mid-Oct, to 7pm late Jul & Aug; P) was transformed into Britain's first safari park in 1966, turning Lancelot 'Capability' Brown's landscaped grounds into an amazing drive-through zoo populated by a menagerie of animals more at home in the African wilderness than the fields of Wiltshire. There's a throng of attractions, too: the historic house,

Stourhead

FABIO REIS/SHUTTERSTOCK ©

Wilton House

Stately **Wilton House** (Map p116, E6; 📞01722-746728; www.wiltonhouse.
co.uk; Wilton; house & grounds adult/child £15.50/13.25; ⏱11.30am-5pm
Sun-Thu May-Sep; 🅿) provides an insight into the rarefied world of
the British aristocracy. One of England's finest stately homes, it's
been the house of the earls of Pembroke since 1542, and has been
expanded and improved by successive generations. Highlights are
the Single and Double Cube Rooms, designed by the pioneering
17th-century architect Inigo Jones.

The result of centuries of embellishments at Wilton is quite stag-
gering: magnificent period furniture, fresco ceilings and elaborate
plasterwork frame paintings by Van Dyck, Rembrandt and Joshua
Reynolds. All the architectural eye candy makes the house a
favoured film location: *The Madness of King George*, *Sense and
Sensibility* and *Pride and Prejudice* were all shot here. But Wilton
served as an artistic haven long before the movies – famous guests
include Ben Jonson, Edmund Spenser, Christopher Marlowe and
John Donne. Shakespeare's *As You Like It* was performed here in
1603, shortly after the bard had written it.

The 22 acres of parkland and **gardens** (adult/child £6.50/5;
⏱11am-5.30pm May to mid-Sep) of Wilton House are bordered by the
rivers Wylye and Nadder, and were largely laid out by the famous
landscape gardener, Lancelot 'Capability' Brown.

Wilton House is 2.5 miles west of Salisbury; bus R3 runs from Salisbury (£2.70, 10 minutes, one to three hourly Monday to Saturday).

animatronic dinosaur exhibits,
narrow-gauge railway, mazes, pets'
corner, a butterfly garden and a
bat cave. It's just off the A362, 3
miles from Frome. Save around
10% by booking tickets online.

Malmesbury

3 🎯 MAP P116, C1

A blend of ruin and living church,
Malmesbury Abbey (📞01666-
826666; www.malmesburyabbey.info;
suggested donation £5-10; ⏱9am-
5pm Easter-Sep, to 4pm Oct-Easter)
has a somewhat turbulent history.
Notable features include the
Norman doorway decorated with
biblical figures, the Romanesque
Apostle carvings and a four-volume
illuminated bible dating from 1407.
A window at the western end of
the church depicts Elmer the Flying Monk, who in 1010 strapped on
wings and jumped from the tower.
Although he broke both legs during this leap of faith, he survived
and became a local hero.

The beautifully kept, 2-hectare **Abbey House Gardens** (☎01666-827650; www.abbeyhousegardens.co.uk; adult/child £8/4; ☻11am-5.30pm Apr-Sep) feature neatly clipped hedges, a herb garden, a waterfall and colourful English country cottage–style blooms.

Lacock

4 ◎ MAP P116, C2

With its geranium-covered cottages and higgledy-piggledy rooftops, pockets of the medieval village of Lacock seem to have been preserved in mid-19th-century aspic. The village has been in the hands of the National Trust since 1944, and in many places is remarkably free of modern development – there are no telephone poles or electric street lights and the main car park on the outskirts keeps it relatively traffic-free.

Lacock Abbey (NT; ☎01249-730459; www.nationaltrust.org.uk; Hither Way; adult/child £13.40/6.70; ☻10.30am-5.30pm Mar-Oct, 11am-4pm Nov-Feb) is a window into a medieval world. Founded as an Augustinian nunnery in the 13th century, its deeply atmospheric rooms and stunning Gothic entrance hall are lined with bizarre terracotta figures; spot the scapegoat with a lump of sugar on its nose. Some of the original structure is evident in the cloisters and there are traces of medieval wall paintings, too.

Located within the abbey, the **Fox Talbot Museum** details the groundbreaking work of William Henry Fox Talbot (1800–77), who pioneered the photographic negative. A prolific inventor, he began developing the system in 1834 while working at Lacock Abbey. There is a superb collection of his images on display.

When hunger strikes, afternoon tea is a must at Lacock's oldest building, which houses **King John's Hunting Lodge** (☎01249-730313; 21 Church St; snacks from £5; ☻11am-5pm Wed-Sun Feb–mid-Dec; P), where a cosy, beam-lined room and a peaceful garden set the scene for dainty china, light lunches and tasty cakes.

Wadworth Brewery

A must for ale aficionados, this Victorian **brewery** (Map p116, D3; ☎01380-732277; www.wadworthvisitorcentre.co.uk; Northgate St, Devizes; adult/child £12/6; ☻11am & 2pm Mon-Sat) has been producing the tawny elixir since 1875. During a two-hour tour you get to smell the hops, sample the product and visit the brewery's shire horse stables. These colossal creatures still stop traffic in Devizes each day, when they deliver beer to the local pubs by cart. Book in advance.

Ancient Foundations

The oldest surviving structures in England are the grass-covered mounds of earth, called 'tumuli' or 'barrows', used as burial sites by England's prehistoric residents. These mounds – measuring anything from a rough semisphere just 2m high to much larger, elongated semi-ovoids 5m high and 10m long – are dotted across the countryside from Cornwall to Cumbria, and are especially common in chalk areas such as Salisbury Plain and the Wiltshire Downs in southern England.

Perhaps the most famous chalk mound – and certainly the largest and most mysterious – is Silbury Hill (p113), near Marlborough. Archaeologists are not sure exactly why this 40m-high conical mound was built – there's no evidence of it actually being used for burial. Theories suggest it was used in cultural ceremonies or as part of the worship of deities in the style of South American pyramids. Whatever its original purpose, it still remains impressive, more than four millennia after it was built.

Even more impressive than giant tumuli are another legacy of the Neolithic era: menhirs (standing stones), especially when they're set out in rings. These include the iconic stone circle of Stonehenge (p122) and the even larger Avebury Stone Circle (p113), both in Wiltshire. Again, their original purpose is a mystery, providing fertile ground for hypothesis and speculation. The most recent theories suggest Stonehenge may have been a place of pilgrimage for the sick, like modern-day Lourdes, though it was also used as a burial ground and as a place of ancestor worship.

For something more substantial, sample well-executed, classic pub grub and some of the six local ales at the **George Inn** (www.georgeinnlacock.co.uk; 4 West St; mains £8-20; ☀kitchen noon-2.30pm & 6-9pm Mon-Sat, 6-8pm Sun), a 14th-century, horse brass–hung pub.

Top Sights 📷
Stonehenge

Welcome to Britain's most iconic archaeological site. This compelling ring of monolithic stones, located near Amesbury, has been attracting a steady stream of pilgrims, poets and philosophers for the last 5000 years. It's still a mystical, ethereal place – a haunting echo from Britain's forgotten past, and a reminder of those who once walked the ceremonial avenues across Salisbury Plain.

📞 0370 333 1181

www.english-heritage.org.uk

adult/child same-day tickets £19.50/11.70, advance booking £17.50/10.50

🕑 9am-8pm Jun-Aug, 9.30am-7pm Apr, May & Sep, 9.30am-5pm Oct-Mar

Sacred Stones

Stonehenge is one of Britain's great archaeological mysteries: despite countless theories
about the site's purpose, from a sacrificial
centre to a celestial timepiece, no one knows
for sure what drove prehistoric Britons to
expend so much time and effort on its construction, although recent archeological find-
ings show the surrounding area was sacred for
hundreds of years before work began.

Creation

The first phase of building started around
3000 BC, when the outer circular bank and
ditch were erected. A thousand years later,
an inner circle of granite stones, known as
bluestones, was added. It's thought that these
mammoth 4-tonne blocks were hauled from
the Preseli Mountains in South Wales, some
250 miles away – an extraordinary feat for
Stone Age people. Around 1500 BC, Stonehenge's main stones were dragged to the site,
erected in a circle and crowned by massive lin-
tels to make the trilithons (two vertical stones
topped by a horizontal one).

Stone Circle Access Visits

Visitors normally have to stay outside the stone
circle itself, but on these hour-long, self-guided
walks (☎ 0370 333 0605; www.english-heritage.org.
uk; adult/child £38.50/23.10), you get to wander
around the heart of the archaeological site, getting up close. Tours take place in the evening or
early morning. Each visit only takes 30 people;
book at least three months in advance.

Stonehenge Walks

The National Trust (www.nationaltrust.org.
uk) website has a downloadable 3.5-mile
circular walk (search for A Kings View) that
traces tracks across the chalk downland from
Stonehenge.

★ Getting There

No regular buses
go to the site. The
Stonehenge Tour
(www.thestonehenge
tour.info; ☎ 01202-
338420; adult/child/
family £30/20/90)
leaves Salisbury's
railway station half-
hourly from June to
August, and hourly
between September
and May. The ticket
includes entry to
Stonehenge and the
Iron Age hill fort at
Old Sarum (Castle Rd;
⏰10am-6pm Apr-Sep,
to 5pm Oct, to 4pm Nov-
Mar); it stops there on
the return leg.

★ Top Tip

Stonehenge operates
by timed tickets,
meaning if you want
to guarantee your
entry you have to
book in advance. If
you're planning a
peak-season visit,
secure your ticket
well in advance.

✕ Take a Break

The Stonehenge
visitor centre has
a decent cafe –
otherwise consider
bringing your own
picnic supplies.

Explore

Somerset

With its pastoral landscape of hedgerows, fields and hummocked hills, sleepy Somerset is the very picture of rural England. The cathedral city of Wells is an atmospheric base for exploring the limestone caves and gorges around Cheddar, while the hippie haven of Glastonbury is handy for venturing to the Somerset Levels and the high hills of the Quantocks.

Start your day early with a bracing walk up Glastonbury Tor (p127) in the morning light before descending towards the dramatic ruins of Glastonbury Abbey (p127), passing Chalice Well & Gardens (p127) and the White Spring (p128) en route. After admiring the sublime abbey vestiges, pop into the Lake Village Museum (p127) before having lunch at cool Bocabar (p128). In the afternoon, drive to Wells and make sure you have a place booked for the behind-the-scenes tour (p133) of superb Wells Cathedral (p132). Don't overlook the Vicars' Close (p132), with its medieval flavours, before enjoying dinner at nearby Goodfellows Cafe & Seafood Restaurant (p135) or Square Edge (p135).

Getting There & Around

For timetables and general information, contact Traveline South West (www.travelinesw.com).

🚗 The M5 heads south past Bristol to Bridgwater and Taunton, while the A39 leads west across the Quantocks to Exmoor.

🚆 Key train services link Bath, Bristol, Bridgwater, Taunton and Weston-super-Mare.

🚌 First (www.firstgroup.com) is a key local bus operator.

Somerset Map on p130

Wells (p132) IAN WOOLCOCK/SHUTTERSTOCK ©

Top Sights 📷
Glastonbury

Ley lines converge, white witches convene and shops are filled with the aroma of smouldering joss sticks in southwest England's undisputed capital of alternative culture. Famous for its mud-soaked music festival, Glastonbury has an ancient past: its iconic tor was an important pagan site, and is rumoured by some to be the mythical Isle of Avalon, King Arthur's last resting place.

◎ MAP P130, G4

www.visitsomerset.
co.uk/explore-somerset/
glastonbury-p499003

Ancient Landmarks

Topped by the ruined, medieval Chapel of St Michael, the iconic hump of **Glastonbury Tor** (admission free; ⏱24hr) is visible for miles around, and provides Somerset with one of its most unmistakable landmarks. It takes half an hour to walk up from the start of the trail on Well House Lane; the steepest sections are stepped. Between April and September a regular Tor Bus (adult/child £3/1.50) runs every half hour from St Dunstan's car park near Glastonbury Abbey to the trailhead on Well House Lane.

The scattered ruins of **Glastonbury Abbey** (📞01458-832267; www.glastonburyabbey.com; Magdalene St; adult/child £7.50/4.50; ⏱9am-6pm Mar-May, Sep & Oct, to 8pm Jun-Aug, to 4pm Nov-Feb), pictured left, give little hint that this was once one of England's great seats of ecclesiastical power. It was torn down following Henry VIII's dissolution of the monasteries in 1539, and the last abbot, Richard Whiting, was hung, drawn and quartered on the tor. Today's striking ruins include some of the nave walls, the remains of St Mary's chapel, and the crossing arches, which may have been scissor-shaped like those in Wells Cathedral.

Shaded by yew trees and criss-crossed by quiet paths, the **Chalice Well & Gardens** (📞01458-831154; www.chalicewell.org.uk; Chilkwell St; adult/child £4.30/2.15; ⏱10am-6pm Apr-Oct, to 4.30pm Nov-Mar) have been sites of pilgrimage since the days of the Celts. The iron-red waters from the 800-year-old well are rumoured to have healing properties, good for everything from eczema to smelly feet; some legends also identify the well as the hiding place of the Holy Grail.

The **Lake Village Museum** (The Tribunal, 9 High St; adult/child £3.50/2; ⏱10am-3pm Mon-Sat) displays finds from a prehistoric bog village discovered in nearby Godney. The houses were clustered in about six groups and built from

★ Top Tips

○ Glastonbury's **tourist office** (📞01458-832954; www.glastonburytic. co.uk; Magdalene St; ⏱10am-4pm Mon-Sat, 11am-3pm Sun) is in the town hall.

○ There is no train station in Glastonbury.

○ Useful bus routes include Taunton (bus 29; £5.70, 1½ hours, four to seven daily Monday to Saturday) and Wells (bus 376; £3.70, 15 minutes, several times an hour).

reeds, hazel and willow. It's thought they were occupied by summer traders who lived the rest of the year around Glastonbury Tor.

Also visit the sacred well of **White Spring** (Well House Lane), which is said to have healing powers.

Eating & Drinking Highlights

You'll find everything from classic pub grub to organic and vegan offerings.

Psychedelic cafe **Rainbow's End** (📞01458-833896; www.rainbowsendcafe.com; 17b High St; mains £6-9; ⏰10am-4pm; 🍴) sums up the Glastonbury spirit, with its all-veggie food, potted plants and mix-and-match furniture. Tuck into homity pie or a hot quiche, followed by scrumptious homemade cake.

The vegan and gluten-free menu is extensive and there's a small patio out back.

Cavernous red-brick **Bocabar** (📞01458-440558; http://glastonbury.bocabar.co.uk; Morland Rd; mains £8-17; ⏰9.30am-11pm Tue-Thu, to 1am Fri & Sat, 10am-5pm Sun & Mon), a former sheepskin factory, is now a hip hangout. Its pan-global menu takes in mezze platters, fish stews, gourmet burgers and adventurous puddings. Live bands play several times a week, the G&T menu boasts 22 types of gin, and an industrial-chic vibe adds to the appeal.

Buzzy High St bistro **Hundred Monkeys Cafe** (www.hundredmonkeyscafe.com; 52 High St; mains £7-14; ⏰9am-5pm Sun-Wed, to 8.30pm Thu-Sat; 🍴) has a fair-trade, local, seasonal, organic ethos that infuses

Glastonbury Festival

Glastonbury Festival

To many people, Glastonbury is synonymous with the **Glastonbury Festival of Contemporary Performing Arts** (www.glastonburyfestivals. co.uk; tickets from £238; ⏱ Jun or Jul), an iconic event that has blossomed from a gathering of flower power–era happy hippies to one of the biggest, busiest, most bonkers celebrations of music, art, performance and general hipness around.

The first event was held near Glastonbury in 1970, when young dairy farmer Michael Eavis decided to stage his own British version of Woodstock on his land at Worthy Farm. Eavis borrowed £15,000 and invited some bands to play on a couple of makeshift stages in a field. Entry was £1, which included a pint of milk from Eavis' dairy herd; among the performers was Marc Bolan of T-Rex, who arrived in typically flamboyant style in his own velvet-covered Buick.

Almost half a century later, the festival has become the world's longest-running pop-music festival, attracting crowds of more than 120,000. It's even had a feature-length film made about it, directed by Julien Temple. Eavis' daughter Emily has since taken over the day-to-day running of the festival, and her decision to give headline slots to artists such as Dolly Parton, Jay-Z and U2 has led some to grumble that Glastonbury's gone mainstream – but with acts such as the Rolling Stones and the Arctic Monkeys still lining up to play, Glastonbury's status as the UK's premier outdoor party looks safe for years to come.

More importantly, even the local councillors seem to have come around; after years of wrangling, in 2014 the festival was granted an unprecedented 10-year licence, a sign that the powers that be have recognised the festival's status as a national treasure. Tickets usually go on sale in the autumn, and always sell out within a matter of minutes, so you need to get in lightning quick if you want to go.

the mezze platters, pasta dishes, curries and risottos – including plenty of gluten-free and vegan options. The wines are biodynamic and the tea selection is enormous.

Who'd a Thought It Inn (☎ 01458-834460; www.whoda thoughtit.co.uk; 17 Northload St; mains £12-18; ⏱ noon-9.30pm) is a pleasantly peculiar locals' pub. Vintage advertising signs sit beside an old, red telephone box and an upside-down bike dangles from the ceiling. The food here is solid pub fare: sausages, pies and steaks, plus specials chalked above the bar.

In hippy-chic Glastonbury, the **George & Pilgrim** (☎ 01458-831146; www.historicinnz.co.uk; 1 High St; ⏱ 11am-11pm) pub is a rarity: an ancient inn with one of the town's most authentically historic interiors – timbers, flagstones and all.

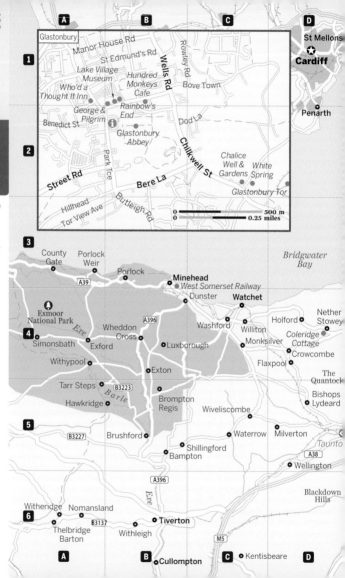

Somerset

N

0   20 km
0   10 miles

Portishead

Severn Estuary

Clevedon

Tyntesfield

Bristol

Flax Bourton

Bristol Airport

A4

Keynsham

M5

A370

A38

Chew Magna

Congresbury

Churchill

Blagdon Lakes

Chew Stroke

A368

Weston-super-Mare

Compton Martin

West Harptree

Midsomer Norton

Radstock

Axbridge

Cheddar 2

A371

Mendip Hills

Chewton Mendip

Burnham-on-Sea

Wedmore

Wookey Hole

A37

A38

Axe

Wells

Shepton Mallet

Combwich

Westhay

Meare

Coxley 1

Glastonbury

A361

Bridgwater

Ashcott

Bocabar

Pedwell

Butleigh

A37

Castle Cary

M5

Othery

Burrowbridge

Langport

Somerton

Haynes Motor Museum

A361

Stoke St Gregory

Long Sutton

A372

Willows & Wetlands Visitor Centre

Curry Rivel

Ilchester

Fleet Air Arm Museum

A303

Martock

Montacute House

South Petherton

Stoke-sub-Hamdon

Ham Hill

Yeovil 4

Sherborne

Barwick

A358

Illminster

Lord Poulett Arms

combwich

A303

Chard

Crewkerne

A37

Wells

1 MAP P130, G3

In Wells, medieval buildings and cobbled streets radiate out from the cathedral green to a marketplace that has been the bustling heart of the city for some nine centuries (Wednesday and Saturday are market days).

This is England's smallest city. It only qualifies for the title thanks to its magnificent medieval cathedral, the gargantuan Gothic **Wells Cathedral** (Cathedral Church of St Andrew; ☎01749-674483; www.wellscathedral.org.uk; Cathedral Green; requested donation adult/child £6/5; ⏱7am-7pm Apr-Sep, to 6pm Oct-Mar), which sits plumb in the centre of the city, surrounded by one of the largest cathedral closes in England. It was built in stages between 1180 and 1508, and consequently showcases several Gothic styles. Among its notable features are the **West Front**, decorated with more than 300 carved figures, and the famous **scissor arches** – an ingenious architectural solution to counter the subsidence of the central tower. Don't miss the High Parts Tour that heads up into the roof.

The cathedral forms the centrepiece of a cluster of ecclesiastical buildings dating back to the Middle Ages. Facing the West Front, on the left are the 15th-century **Old Deanery** and the Wells Museum (p134). Further north, **Vicars' Close** is a stunning 14th-century cobbled street, with a chapel at

West Somerset Railway

The Somerset Levels

Flat as a pancake, sub-sea-level and criss-crossed with canals (known locally as rhynes), the Somerset Levels are one of England's largest native wetlands. Covering almost 250 sq miles between the Quantock and Mendip Hills, they're brilliant for bird-spotters – particularly in October and November, when huge flocks of starlings (properly known as murmurations) descend on the area. Nature reserves have been established at Ham Wall, Shapwick Heath, Sedgemoor and Westhay.

The flat landscape of the Levels also makes it ideal for cycling. Several trails pass through the village of Langport, including the long-distance River Parrett Trail.

the end; members of the cathedral choir still live here. It is thought to be the oldest complete medieval street in Europe.

Contact **High Parts Tour** (☏01749-674483; www.wellscathedral.org.uk; Wells Cathedral, Cathedral Green; adult/child £10/8; ☉Mon-Sat May-Oct) for a 1½-hour behind-the-scenes tour of Wells Cathedral. You'll clamber up spiral staircases, explore the transept's roof space and discover a hidden singing gallery and the chamber behind the Wells clock. Places are limited; be sure to book in advance online.

Beside the cathedral sits the grand **Bishop's Palace** (☏01749-988111; www.bishopspalace.org.uk; Market Pl; adult/child £8/4; ☉10am-6pm Apr-Oct, to 4pm Nov-Mar), the official residence of the Bishop of Bath and Wells since it was constructed in the 13th century. This moat-ringed palace is purportedly the oldest inhabited building in England. Inside, the palace's state rooms and ruined great hall are worth a look, but it's the shady gardens that are the real draw. The natural springs after which Wells is named bubble up in the palace's grounds.

West Somerset Railway

The steam trains of this vintage **railway** (Map p130, B3; ☏01643-704996; www.west-somerset-railway.co.uk; 24hr rover tickets adult/child £20/10) are a fine way to see the Somerset countryside. The 20-mile route runs from its base at Minehead to Bishops Lydeard, stopping at Dunster, Watchet, Williton, Crowcombe Heathfield and several other stations en route. There are four to seven trains daily from May to October, with a more limited service in March, April and December.

Tyntesfield

Formerly the home of the Gibbs family, **Tyntesfield** (Map p130, G1; 01275-461900; www.nationaltrust.org.uk/tyntesfield; Wraxall; adult/child £15.60/7.80, gardens only £9.60/4.80; house 11am-5pm Mar-Oct, 11am-3pm Nov-Feb, gardens 10am-5pm year-round) was purchased by the National Trust in 2002. A fairy-tale mansion bristling with pinnacles and turrets, brimful of sweeping staircases and cavernous, antique-filled rooms, the house gives an insight into the lavish lives once enjoyed by England's wealthiest families.

Built in grand Gothic Revival style by the architect John Norton, it was in danger of collapse when the trust acquired it, but has since undergone extensive (and very expensive) renovations. Outside, work continues on the orangery and walled gardens.

Entry is via timed ticket and includes a guided tour. The house is 8 miles southwest of Bristol, off the B3128.

Exhibits at **Wells Museum** (01749-673477; www.wellsmuseum.org.uk; 8 Cathedral Green; adult/child £3/1; 10am-5pm Mon-Sat Easter-Oct, to 4pm Nov-Easter) include those on local life, cathedral architecture and archaeological finds from the nearby cave network of Wookey Hole, including the bones of the infamous 'Witch of Wookey Hole'. The most striking display, though, is the 2m-long skeleton of an ichthyosaur in the lobby.

Three miles northwest of Wells on the A371, follow the brown tourist signs to **Wookey Hole** (01749-672243; www.wookey.co.uk; adult/child £19/15; 10am-5pm Apr-Oct, to 4pm Nov-Mar). Here, the River Axe has gouged out a network of deep limestone caverns, which are famous for striking stalagmites and stalactites, one of which is the legendary Witch of Wookey

Hole who, it's said, was turned to stone by a local priest. Admission to the caves is by guided tour; up on top you'll find 20 beyond-kitsch attractions ranging from animatronic dinosaurs to pirate adventure golf.

Wells has some good eateries and some charming cafes.

The views from award-winning **Bishop's Table** (01749-988111; www.bishopspalace.org.uk; Bishop's Palace, Market Pl; snacks from £4; 10am-6pm Apr-Oct, to 4pm Nov-Mar;) are often of a quintes-sentially English scene: croquet players, dressed all in white, tapping their way around the lawns of the Bishop's Palace. An irresistible setting for breakfast and lunch, packed with ethical, local produce, strong coffee and sticky cakes.

'Life is too short to drink bad coffee' says the sign – something they've taken to heart here at **Strangers with Coffee** (☎07728 047233; 31 St Cuthbert St; cakes £3-5; ☻7.30am-4pm Tue-Sat) as staff work caffeinated magic with some of the best beans in town. There's a tempting selection of cakes to match.

Good Earth (☎01749-678600; www.thegoodearthwells.co.uk; 6 Priory Rd; mains £9-14; ☻9am-4.30pm Mon-Fri, to 5pm Sat;) is a wholefoods shop that has branched out into homewares and a fantastic veggie cafe. It offers two daily dishes plus salads, soups, pizzas and quiches, to be enjoyed in a sunny dining room or the secret patio garden.

There's a choice of eating options in the three vibrant rooms at **Goodfellows Cafe & Seafood Restaurant** (☎01749-673866; www.goodfellowswells.co.uk; 5 Sadler St; mains £11-24; ☻10am-3pm daily, 6-9.30pm Wed-Sat): the continental cafe menu offers cakes, pastries and light lunches (opt to pay either £11 or £20 for two courses and a drink). Or book for an evening fine-dining experience: £30 gets you three classy courses, while the five-course seafood tasting menu (£50) is an absolute treat.

There's an easygoing charm to **Square Edge** (☎01749-671166; www.square-edgecafe.co.uk; 2 Town Hall Bldgs; mains £7-12; ☻9am-5pm Mon-Sat, 10am-4pm Sun), a retro eatery where 1950s movie posters frame old jukeboxes and

Tyntesfield

vintage radios. Treats range from full-blown cooked breakfasts and American pancakes to tangy salt beef toasties and slow-cooked ribs. The cakes are creative and great.

Cheddar

2 ⊙ MAP P130, F3

Carved out by glacial meltwater during the last ice age, the limestone cliffs of **Cheddar Gorge** (🕿 01934-742343; www.cheddargorge. co.uk; adult/child £20/15; ⊙10am-5pm) form England's deepest natural canyon, in places towering 138m above the twisting B3135. The gorge is riddled with subterranean caverns with impressive displays of stalactites and stalagmites. The easiest to reach are **Gough's Cave** and **Cox's Cave** (the latter, now branded Dreamhunters, features multimedia displays on prehistoric peoples). Admission covers parking and entry to the caves. Cheddar Gorge is 20 miles northwest of Wells on the A371.

The Cheddar Gorge's main outdoors company **Rocksport** (🕿 01934-742343; www.cheddargorge. co.uk/rocksport; adult/child £22/20) offers guided caving trips lasting around 1½ hours. Crawling, climbing ladders and squeezing through small spaces inevitably means you'll get wet and dirty. But that photo featuring mud-caked dungarees, helmet and head torch is worth it. Rocksport also runs rock-climbing sessions (adult/child £22/20).

Cheddar Cheese

Cheddar, a village 10 miles northwest of Wells, is famous for its caves, and as the spiritual home of the nation's favourite cheese. Cheddar's strong, crumbly, tangy cheese is the essential ingredient in any self-respecting ploughman's lunch, and has been produced in the area since at least the 12th century. Henry II boldly proclaimed Cheddar to be 'the best cheese in Britain', and the king's accounts from 1170 record that he purchased 10,240lbs (around 4644kg) of the stuff.

In the days before refrigeration, the Cheddar caves made the ideal cool store for the cheese, with a constant temperature of around 7°C. However, the powerful smell attracted rats and the practice was eventually abandoned.

These days most Cheddar cheese is made far from the village, but if you're interested in seeing how the genuine article is made, head for the Cheddar Gorge Cheese Company.

Coleridge Cottage

The poet Samuel Taylor Coleridge moved to this 17th-century **cottage** (Map p130, D4; ☏ 01278-732662; www.nationaltrust.org.uk; 35 Lime St; adult/child £6.60/3.30; ☉ 11am-5pm Mar-Oct) with his wife Sara and son Hartley in 1796. It's where he's thought to have composed some of his greatest works, including 'The Rime of the Ancient Mariner', 'Kubla Khan' and 'This Lime-Tree Bower My Prison'. An atmospheric restoration and audio installations create the sense that the poet has just popped out for a stroll. It's in the village of Nether Stowey, 12 miles north of Taunton.

At the **Cheddar Gorge Cheese Company** (☏ 01934-742810; www.cheddargorgecheeseco.co.uk; The Cliffs; adult/child £2/free; ☉ 10am-5pm Easter-Oct, winter hours vary) you can watch the whole creamy, gooey transformation process from a viewing gallery, sample the produce, then buy some tangy, whiffy souvenirs at the shop. If you want to see the cheesemaking in progress, get here before around 2.45pm.

Taunton

3 ◉ **MAP P130, D5**

Taunton is in the heart of Somerset in more ways than one; it's bang in the middle of the county geographically, and is the area's county town and commercial centre. It's also a useful gateway to the Quantocks (p139).

Somerset's main county museum, the **Museum of Somerset** (☏ 01823-255088; www.museumofsomerset.org.uk; Castle Green; admission free; ☉ 10am-5pm Tue-Sat), is housed in the great hall of Taunton's 12th-century castle. The highlight is the Frome Hoard, an enormous haul of 52,500 Roman coins that was discovered in a Somerset field in 2010. Also look out for the beautiful *Low Ham Mosaic* (which depicts the story of Dido and Aeneas and was found in a nearby Roman villa), and the specially commissioned *Tree of Somerset*, an oak sculpture depicting local historical events.

Ten miles east of Taunton, **Willows & Wetlands Visitor Centre** (☏ 01823-490249; www.englishwillowbaskets.co.uk; Meare Green Court, near Stoke St Gregory; adult/child £4.50/3; ☉ 9.30am-5pm Mon-Sat) provides a chance to chart the course of the ancient willow industry, from reed harvesting and willow drying to the making of baskets. For deeper insights, especially into the Somerset Levels' environmental importance, join an hour-long guided tour (11am and 2.30pm, Monday to Friday).

Around Yeovil

4 👁 MAP P130, G6

There are a few sights worth a visit in the area around the village of Yeovil.

Built in the 1590s for Sir Edward Phelips, a speaker of the House of Commons, **Montacute House** (NT; 📞 01935-823289; www.nationaltrust. org.uk; Montacute; adult/child £12/6; 🕒 house 11am-4pm Mar-Oct, 11am-3pm Nov & Dec, noon-3pm Sat & Sun Jan-Feb, gardens 10am-5pm Mar-Oct, 11am-4pm Wed-Sat Nov-Feb) contains some of the finest 16th- and 17th-century interiors in the country. Its plasterwork, chimney pieces and tapestries are renowned, but the highlight is the Long Gallery – the longest such hall in England, and rich in Elizabethan portraits. Montacute is 5 miles west of Yeovil off the A3088.

Fleet Air Arm Museum (📞 01963-840565; www.fleetairarm. com; RNAS Yeovilton, Ilchester; adult/child £16/12; 🕒 10am-5.30pm daily Apr-Oct, to 4.30pm Wed-Sun Nov-Mar) is an excellent aviation museum

Quantocks

7 miles north of Yeovil. It houses hundreds of naval aircraft, from a Sea Fury to Phantom fighters. You can walk on to the flight deck of the first British-built Concorde and take a simulated flight on to the aircraft carrier HMS *Ark Royal*.

The 400-strong collection at the **Haynes Motor Museum**

Lord Poulett Arms

At Hinton St George's deliciously olde-worlde village **pub** (Map p130, F6; 📞 01460-73149; www.lordpoulettarms.com; High St; mains £15-26; 🕒 noon-2pm & 6-9pm; P) the assured food pairs classic ingredients with imaginative additions – here prime meat and fish come with wild-garlic pesto, chipotle mayonnaise and horseradish crème fraîche. The building oozes country atmosphere, with beams, roaring fires and stacks of ale barrels behind the bar. Hard to fault. It's roughly 15 miles from Yeovil and Taunton.

The Quantocks

The range of red sandstone hills known as the Quantocks traces a 12-mile curve across Somerset's northern edge. A mix of moors, valleys and ancient woods of coppiced oak, these little-visited hills offer stirring views across the Bristol Channel: when the weather's fine, you can see across to the Gower coastline in South Wales.

Designated as an Area of Outstanding Natural Beauty (AONB), the Quantocks receive far fewer visitors than Exmoor and Dartmoor, making them perfect for hikers and bikers in search of quiet trails.

(01963-440804; www.haynes motormuseum.com; near Sparkford; adult/child £14.50/9; ⏰9.30am-5.30pm Mar-Oct, to 4.30pm Nov-Feb) includes an array of outstanding and outlandish motors, from Aston Martins and Ferraris to oddities such as the Sinclair C5. Don't miss the Red Room, famous for its collection of scarlet cars. The museum is 10 miles northeast of Yeovil, off the A303.

Looming above the village of Stoke-sub-Hamdon, 7 miles west of Yeovil off the A303/A3088, **Ham Hill** (www.southsomerset.gov. uk/hamhill; admission free) is the highest point in Somerset. It's served a variety of purposes – Iron Age hill fort, medieval village, stone quarry – and it's now a delightful park covering 390 acres. Recent archaeological excavations have revealed a huge Iron Age bone pit.

Survival Guide

Bath Bus Station (p144) DRIMAFILM/SHUTTESTOCK ©

Before You Go

Book Your Stay

Useful Websites

Visit Bath (www.visitbath.co.uk) Official tourist website listing 150 hotels, B&Bs and self-catering options.

The Bath Guide (www.thebathguide.com) Database of around 160 accommodation options.

Visit Bristol (www.visitbristol.co.uk) Official tourist website featuring hundreds of hotels, B&Bs and serviced apartments.

Lonely Planet (lonelyplanet.com/hotels) Recommendations and bookings.

Best Budget

Kyle Blue (📞 0117-929 0609; www.kylebluebristol.co.uk; Wapping Wharf; dm/s/d £29/52/59; 📶) Water traffic drifts past the dorm windows of this smart Bristol harbourside hostel boat.

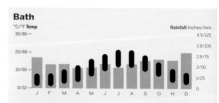

Bath

°C/°F Temp   Rainfall Inches/mm

When to Go

o **High Season (Jun–Aug)** The weather's at its best and there's a holiday vibe, but the sights can get crowded and accommodation is at its most expensive.

o **Shoulder Season (Mar–May, Sep–Oct)** Spring and autumn are lower-key versions of summer with some of the benefits but not the crowds.

o **Low Season (Nov–Feb)** Rates for B&Bs and hotels are at their lowest. Some sights and attractions close or operate shorter hours.

Bristol YHA (📞 0345 371 9726; www.yha.org.uk; 14 Narrow Quay; dm £15-35, d £59-90; @ 📶) Superbly central and modern rooms plus a cool cafe-bar.

Rock n' Bowl (📞 0117-325 1980; www.thelanesbristol.co.uk/hostel; 22 Nelson St; dm £15-36, d £45-65; 📶) Street art covers the walls of this rambling, grungy Bristol hostel, set above a vintage bowling alley.

Best Midrange

Three Abbey Green (📞 01225-428558; www.threeabbeygreen.com; 3 Abbey Green; s £108-144, d £120-200, q £240; 📶) Historic, friendly and superbly central place in Bath.

Brooks (📞 0117-930 0066; www.brooksguesthousebristol.com; Exchange Ave; d £67-120, tr £90-129, trailers £80-149; 📶) A sleek, supremely central Bristol B&B with a surprise on the roof: a clutch of vintage airstream trailers.

Covenstead (📞 01458-830278; www.covenstead.co.uk; Magdalene St; s £70, d £80-110; P 📶) Wacky but fun and wonderful Glastonbury B&B.

Hill House Bath

(☎ 01225-920520; www.hillhousebath.co.uk; 25 Belvedere; r £115-135; P 🛜) Designer flair and great breakfasts in Bath.

Appletree (☎ 01225-337642; www.appletreebath.com; 7 Pulteney Gardens; r £95-165; P 🛜) Calm, quiet and classy with an Asian feel, in Bath.

Manor Farm (☎ 01672-539294; www.manorfarmavebury.com; High St; s/d £90/100; P 🛜) Sleep within a stone circle in Avebury.

Mercure Bristol Brigstow (☎ 0117-929 1030; www.mercure.com; 5 Welsh Back; s £85-125, d £90-210; ❄ 🛜) Set plum on the harbour, the pricier rooms have water views.

Sign of the Angel

(☎ 01249-730230; www.signoftheangel.co.uk; 6 Church St; s £110, d £110-140; P 🛜) Fabulous 15th-century charm in Lacock.

Mercure Bristol Grand Hotel (☎ 0871 376 9042; www.mercure.com/gb/hotel-A012-mercure-bristol-grand-hotel/index.shtml; Broad St; d

£115; P 🔄 ❄ 🛜 ❄) A modern refurb of this city-centre, historic hotel adds to its appeal.

Best Top End

Queensberry

(☎ 01225-447928; www.thequeensberry.co.uk; 4 Russell St; r £112-290, ste £250-460; P 🛜) Bath Heritage-chic with a dash of wit.

Haringtons (☎ 01225-461728; www.haringtonshotel.co.uk; 8 Queen St; r £135-200; 🛜) Ditches Bath's period predilection for snazzy modern decor.

Babington House

(☎ 01373-812266; www.babingtonhouse.co.uk; Babington; r £255-380; P 🛜 ❄) Supremely luxurious; situated in Somerset.

Chapter House

(☎ 01722-341277; www.thechapterhouseuk.com; 9 St Johns St; s £115-145 d £135-155; 🛜) All low-hanging beams and wood panels, in Salisbury.

Grays Bath (☎ 01225-403020; www.graysbath.co.uk; 9 Upper Oldfield Park; r £115-245; P 🛜) A wealth of themed styling means you'll find a room to suit.

Number 38 (☎ 0117-946 6905; www.number38clifton.com; 38 Upper Belgrave Rd; s £115, d £125-180, ste £220; P 🛜) Bristol's best sleep spot: a luxury B&B set on the fringes of the Clifton Downs, boasting broad city views.

Hotel du Vin (☎ 0117-403 2979; www.hotelduvin.com; Narrow Lewins Mead; d £139-164, ste £205-270; P ❄ 🛜) Hip, historic and packed full of spoil-yourself touches; in Bristol.

Leighton Townhouse

(☎ 01225-314769; www.leightontownhouse.co.uk; 139 Wells Rd; r £125-170; P ❄ 🛜) Boutique style and luxurious bathroom; in Bath.

Arriving in Bath, Bristol & the Southwest

Bristol Airport

Bristol Airport (Map p130, G2; ☎ 0371 334 4444; www.bristolairport.co.uk) is

located 8 miles from Bristol and 20 miles from Bath. Destinations in Great Britain and Ireland include Aberdeen, Belfast, Edinburgh, Cork, Glasgow and Newcastle (mainly handled by easyJet). Direct links with cities in mainland Europe include those to Barcelona, Berlin, Milan and Paris. Linked to Bristol by the Bristol Airport Flyer (http://flyer.bristolairport.co.uk; single adult/child £7/5, half-hourly, 30 minutes) and taxi (£30, one way). Linked to Bath by bus (adult/child single £14/8, two per hour, 50 minutes) and taxi (£50, one way).

Bath Spa Train Station

Services at this station (Map p38, F5) are regular and reliable, although some intercity ones require a change at Bristol. Direct connections include those to London Paddington (from £35, 90 minutes, half-hourly), Cardiff Central (£21, one hour, hourly) and Bristol (£8, 15 minutes, half-hourly).

The train station is a 400m walk from the centre of town. A taxi rank is outside, with a fare to the city centre costing around £8. Bus U1 runs from the nearby bus station to the edge of the city centre (£2.50).

Bristol Temple Meads Train Station

Services are fast and reliable. Direct connections include those to Bath (£8, 15 minutes, half-hourly), London Paddington (from £35, 90 minutes, half-hourly), Birmingham (£30, 90 minutes, hourly) and Edinburgh (£90, 6½ hours, hourly). The train station is a mile east of the centre of town. Bus 8 (£1.50) runs from Bristol Temple Meads train station to the city centre and onto Clifton every 15 minutes.

Bath Bus Station

Bath's bus and coach station (Map p38, E5) is near the train station.

National Express (www.nationalexpress.com) coaches run direct to the following:

Bristol (£5, 45 minutes, two daily)

London (£20, 2½ hours, hourly)

London Heathrow (£25, three hours, two-hourly)

Services to many other destinations change at Bristol.

The city centre is around 400m north. The U1 bus heads there from outside the station every 20 minutes (£2.50). A taxi fare should cost around £8.

Bristol Bus Station

Bristol's bus station (Map p78, F1) is 500m north of the city centre. Intercity links through National Express (www.nationalexpress.com) are cheaper than the train:

Bath (£5, 45 minutes, two daily)

London (£18, 2½ hours, hourly)

London Heathrow (£30, three hours, two-hourly)

Plymouth (£14, three hours, seven daily)

Getting Around

Bus

Bath Good services, especially between the centre and outlying areas. The old-city core is pedestrianised, which can make routes circuitous – sometimes it's quicker to walk.

Bristol Fast, reliable services, especially between the centre and Clifton. The M2 MetroBus (www.metrobusbristol.co.uk; single £1.50) provides efficient links between Bristol Temple Meads train station, Long Ashton Park & Ride, the city centre and the SS *Great Britain*.

Somerset First (www.firstgroup.com) is a key local bus operator.

Wiltshire Bus coverage can be patchy, especially in the northwest. First (www.firstgroup.com) serves west Wiltshire.

Salisbury Reds (www.salisburyreds.co.uk) covers Salisbury and many rural areas; offers one-day Rover Tickets (adult/child £8.50/5.50) and seven-day passes (Salisbury area £14.50, network-wide £25).

Stagecoach (www.stagecoachbus.com) provides services around Swindon and Salisbury.

Bicycle

Bath is a picturesque option for cycling, but expect some hills. In Bristol, an appealing option is around the harbourside area – the wider city is hilly.

Boat

Bristol Ferry Boat Company (Map p78, E4; ☎ 0117-927 3416; www.bristolferry.com) boats leave roughly hourly from the dock at Cannon's Rd near the tourist office. Its Hotwells service runs west, with stops including Millennium Sq and the SS *Great Britain*, while the Temple Meads service runs east, with stops including Welsh Back, Castle Park (for Cabot Circus) and Temple Meads (for the train station). Fares depend on distance travelled; an all-day pass is £6.50/5.50 per adult/child.

Car & Motorcycle

Bath has serious traffic problems, especially at rush hour. **Park & Ride** (☎ 01225-394041; ⏰ 6.15am-8.30pm Mon-Sat, 9.30am-6pm Sun; return Mon-Fri £3.40, Sat & Sun £3) services operate from Lansdown to the north, Newbridge to the west and Odd Down to the south. It takes about 10 minutes to the centre; buses leave every 10 to 15 minutes. There's a good, central car park underneath the SouthGate shopping centre (two/eight hours £3.50/11).

Heavy traffic and pricey parking make driving in Bristol a headache. Park & Ride buses run approximately every 15 to 20 minutes from Portway, Bath Rd and Long Ashton. Note that overnight parking is not allowed at the Park & Ride car parks.

Taxi

In Bath, taxi ranks include those outside the train station, at Parade Gardens and at the western end of Westgate St. **Bath Taxi** (☎ 0845 003 5205) provides a 24-hour service.

In Bristol you can usually find a cab at the taxi ranks at the train and bus stations and on St Augustine's Pde. To phone for a cab, try **Streamline Taxis** (☎ 0117-926 4001) or **1st Call Taxi** (☎ 0117-955 5111). If you're taking a nonmetered cab, agree on the fare in advance.

Essential Information

Business Hours

Opening hours often vary throughout the year for sights and activities, with many operating shorter hours from October to March, and some shutting down altogether during the winter.

Banks 9.30am to 4pm or 5pm Monday to Friday; possibly 9.30am to 1pm Saturday.

Pubs & bars Noon to 11pm Monday to Saturday (some till midnight or up to 3am Friday and Saturday), 12.30pm to 11pm Sunday.

Restaurants Noon to 2.30pm or 3pm and 6pm to 9pm or 10pm.

Shops 9am to 5.30pm or 6pm Monday to Saturday, normally 11am to 5pm Sunday.

Discount Cards

Bath

Bath Reward Card (www.stayinbath.org/reward-card) Offers discounts when staying with 100 independent accommodation providers, including money off sights, meals and haircuts, and a free extra hour of spa sessions at Thermae Bath Spa.

GWR Offers Visitors travelling by GWR trains can claim nine two-for-one offers, extended spa sessions and discounts on comedy club tickets and sights admission. See www.visitbath.co.uk/special-offers.

Bristol

Bristol has no specific visitor discount cards, but students and pensioners get concessionary rates at attractions and entertainment venues when presenting a valid ID. Students also get discounts from many city shops and services.

GWR Offers Travelling by GWR trains opens up a small selection of discounts, including two-for-one offers at the We the Curious science centre and Bristol Zoo. See www.gwr.com/destinations-and-events.

Dos & Don'ts

○ Good manners matter. When asking directions, 'Excuse me, can you tell me the way to...' is better than 'Hey, where's...'

○ In England, queuing ('standing in line') is sacrosanct, whether to board a bus, buy tickets at a kiosk or enter the gates of an attraction. Any attempt to 'jump the queue' will result in some stern looks.

Electricity

Type G
230V/50Hz

LGBTIQ+ Travellers

Bath echoes many places in Britain as being a generally tolerant place for LGBTIQ+ travellers. However, the city's gay scene is far from flourishing and nearby Bristol has more venues.

Many eateries, nightspots and accommodation providers won't have an issue with your sexuality, although as elsewhere you might still find pockets of homophobic hostility.

Resources include the following:

Diva (www.divamag.co.uk)

Gay Times (www.gaytimes.co.uk)

GayWest (www.gaywest.org.uk) Social and support group covering Bath, Bristol and the surrounding area.

Switchboard LGBT+ Helpline (www.switchboard.lgbt; ☎0300 330 0630)

Money

ATMs are widely available and credit cards widely accepted.

Exchange Rates

Australia	A$1	£0.57
Canada	C$1	£0.57
Eurozone	€1	£0.87
Japan	Y100	£0.65
New Zealand	NZ$1	£0.51
USA	US$1	£0.70

For current exchange rates, see www.xe.com.

Cash

The currency of Britain is the pound sterling (£). Paper money (notes) comes in £5, £10, £20 and £50 denominations. Some shops don't accept £50 notes because fakes circulate.

Other currencies are very rarely accepted, though a handful of enterprising gift shops may take euros or US dollars.

ATMs

ATMs (locally called 'cash machines') are common in central Bath. Cash withdrawals from some ATMs may be subject to a small charge, but most are free to use (look for the 'free cash' sign). However, if you're not from the UK, your home bank will likely charge you for withdrawing money overseas.

Watch out for tampered ATMs; one ruse by scammers is to attach a card-reader or minicamera.

Credit & Debit Cards

Visa and MasterCard are widely accepted, except at some smaller B&Bs, which take cash or cheque only. Other credit cards, including Amex, are not so widely accepted. Most businesses will assume your card is 'Chip and PIN' enabled (using a PIN instead of signing). If it isn't, you should be able to sign instead, but some places may not accept your card.

Changing Money

Banks and exchange bureaux will change your money into pounds. Check rates first; some bureaux offer poor rates or levy hefty commissions. Note you can also change money at bigger post offices, where exchange rates are fair.

Tipping

In England you're not obliged to tip if the service or food was unsatisfactory (even if it's been automatically added to your bill as a 'service charge').

Restaurants Around 10% in restaurants and cafes with table service, 15% at smarter restaurants. Tips may be added to your bill as a 'service charge' – it's not compulsory to pay.

Pubs & Bars Not expected if you order drinks (or food) and pay at the bar; usually 10% if you order at the table and your meal is brought to you.

Taxis Usually 10%, or rounded up to the nearest pound.

Public Holidays

New Year's Day 1 January

Easter March/April (Good Friday to Easter Monday inclusive)

May Day First Monday in May

Spring Bank Holiday Last Monday in May

Summer Bank Holiday Last Monday in August

Christmas Day 25 December

Boxing Day 26 December

Safe Travel

Bath and Bristol are generally safe places, but crime is not unknown. Like most English towns and cities, central areas can be rowdy on Friday and Saturday nights when the pubs and clubs are emptying.

In Bath, avoid wandering alone at night around the city's green spaces, such as Parade Gardens. Keep a close eye on bags and purses amid the tourist crush in the area around the Roman Baths.

In Bristol, be aware after dark of the risks of vehicle and public order crimes in the streets and lanes around the harbourside, Frogmore St and Corn St in particular.

Away from the centre, it's worth taking care around Cheltenham Rd and the districts of St Paul's, Easton and Montpelier.

Toilets

Public toilets are generally clean and modern. Museums, bigger stores and the bus and railway stations also have facilities. Most public toilets are free, some charge a small fee (from 20p to 50p). Pubs and restaurants tend to stipulate that their toilets are for customers only.

Tourist Information

Bath Tourist Office

(Map p38, E3; ☎ 01225-614420; www.visitbath.co.uk; 2 Terrace Walk; ⏱ 9.30am-5.30pm Mon-Sat, 10am-4pm Sun, closed Sun Nov-Jan) Offers advice and information. Also runs an accommodation booking service and sells a wide range of local books and maps.

Bristol Tourist Office

(Map p78, E4; ☎ 0333 321 0101; www.visitbristol.co.uk; E-Shed, 1 Canons Rd; ⏱ 10am-5pm; 📶) Offers information and advice, plus free wi-fi, accommodation bookings and luggage storage (£5 per item).

Isle of Wight Tourist Office

(☎ 01983-813813; www.visitisleofwight.co.uk; High St; ⏱ 9.30am-3.30pm Mon-Fri) In Newport.

Salisbury Tourist Office

(Map p109; ☎ 01722-342860; www.visitsalisbury.co.uk; Fish Row; ⏱ 9am-5pm Mon-Fri, 10am-4pm Sat, 10am-2pm Sun; 📶) Located north of the cathedral.

Taunton Tourist Office

(☎ 01823-340470; www.visitsomerset.co.uk/taunton; Market House, Fore St; ⏱ 9.30am-4.30pm Mon-Sat) The best source of information about Somerset as a whole.

Visas

Generally not needed for stays of up to six months. England is not a member of the Schengen Zone.

o If you're a citizen of the European Economic Area (EEA) nations or Switzerland, you don't need a visa to enter or work in the UK – you can enter using your national identity card.

o Visa regulations are always subject to change, and immigration restriction is big news in the UK, so it's essential to check with your local British embassy, high commission or consulate before leaving home.

o At the time of research, if you're a citizen of Australia, Canada, New Zealand, Japan, Israel, the USA or several other countries, you can stay for up to six months (no visa required), but you are not allowed to work.

o Nationals of many countries, including South Africa, will need to obtain a visa. For more info, see www.gov.uk/check-uk-visa.

o The Youth Mobility Scheme (www.gov.uk/tier-5-youth-mobility), for Australian, Canadian, Japanese, Hong Kong, Monégasque, New Zealand, South Korean and Taiwanese citizens aged 18 to 30, allows working visits of up to two years, but must be applied for in advance.

o Commonwealth citizens with a UK-born parent may be eligible for a Certificate of Entitlement to the Right of Abode, which entitles them to live and work in the UK.

o Commonwealth citizens with a UK-born grandparent could qualify for a UK Ancestry Employment Certificate, allowing them to work full time for up to five years in the UK.

o British immigration authorities have always been tough; dress neatly and carry proof that you have sufficient funds with which to support yourself. A credit card and/or an onward ticket will help.

Entry & Exit Formalities

Entering or leaving the UK is usually straightforward and hassle-free, save for the occasional inconvenience of long queues at passport control and security.

A referendum result in the UK in June 2016 that favoured withdrawal from the EU renders information in this section highly liable to change; it's important to check the current regulations before travel.

Behind the Scenes

Send Us Your Feedback

We love to hear from travellers – your comments help make our books better. We read every word, and we guarantee that your feedback goes straight to the authors. Visit **lonelyplanet.com/contact** to submit your updates and suggestions.

Note: We may edit, reproduce and incorporate your comments in Lonely Planet products such as guidebooks, websites and digital products, so let us know if you don't want your comments reproduced or your name acknowledged. For a copy of our privacy policy visit lonelyplanet.com/privacy.

Damian's Thanks

Many thanks to Ann Harper, Jasmin Tonge, Kevin and Maki Fallows, Rosemary Hadow, Lily Greensmith, Antonia Mavromatidou, Arabella Sneddon, Bill Moran, Jim Peake, my ever-helpful co-authors and a big debt of gratitude again to Daisy, Tim and Emma.

Belinda's Thanks

Researching and writing for Lonely Planet is a real joint effort – so huge thanks to the locals who share their time, knowledge and recommendations and to the random strangers who offer countless kindnesses. And thank you to Cliff for the gig, Lonely Planet's behind the scenes teams (so much work!), and fellow writers for humour, wisdom and travellers' tales.

Oliver's Thanks

As always I've thoroughly enjoyed exploring my homeland for this update, and I'd like to extend a big thanks to everyone who's helped me along the way (you

This Book

This 1st edition of Lonely Planet's *Pocket Bath, Bristol & the Southwest* guidebook was curated by Damian Harper and researched and written by Belinda Dixon and Oliver Berry. This guidebook was produced by the following:

Destination Editors James Smart, Clifton Wilkinson

Senior Product Editor Genna Patterson

Regional Senior Cartographer Mark Griffiths

Product Editors Carolyn Boicos, Jessica Ryan

Book Designer Gwen Cotter

Assisting Editors Judith Bamber, Janice Bird, Kellie Langdon, Rachel Rawling

Assisting Cartographers Mick Garrett, Rachel Imeson

Cover Researcher Naomi Parker

Thanks to Liz Heynes, Martine Power

know who you are). I'd particularly like to thank all my co-authors for their hard work and help, and Cliff Wilkinson for sage advice, feedback and generally keeping the England ship on course. A special thanks also to Rosie Hillier for supporting me, putting up with long days and nights spent at the computer and providing emergency cups of tea when they were most needed.

Acknowledgements

Cover photograph: Roman baths, Bath, Ollie Taylor/Shutterstock ©

Photographs pp28–9 (clockwise): Lou Armor/Claudio Divizia/1000 Words/Nussar/Ian Woolcock/Shutterstock ©

Index

See also separate subindexes for:

⊗ Eating p155
⊖ Drinking p156
☆ Entertainment p156
🔒 Shopping p156

Sights 000
Map Pages 000